Robert Brown

The myth of Kirke: Including a visit of Odysseus to the shades

An Homerik study

Robert Brown

The myth of Kirke: Including a visit of Odysseus to the shades
An Homerik study

ISBN/EAN: 9783337197919

Printed in Europe, USA, Canada, Australia, Japan

Cover: Foto ©Andreas Hilbeck / pixelio.de

More available books at **www.hansebooks.com**

THE

MYTH OF KIRKÊ

INCLUDING

THE VISIT OF ODYSSEUS TO THE SHADES.

AN HOMERIK STUDY.

BY

ROBERT BROWN, Jun., F.S.A.

AUTHOR OF 'THE GREAT DIONYSIAK MYTH,' 'LANGUAGE, AND THEORIES
OF ITS ORIGIN,' 'THE UNICORN,' 'THE LAW OF KOSMIC ORDER,'
'ERIDANUS, RIVER AND CONSTELLATION,' ETC.

'Who knows not Circe
The daughter of the Sun?'

MILTON.

LONDON:

LONGMANS, GREEN, AND CO.

1883.

TO THE MEMORY OF MY MOTHER.

'I mused in my heart and would fain have embraced
the spirit of my Mother dead. . . . . . . And sharper ever
waxed the grief within me.'

Od. xi. 204–5, 208.

FOREWORD.

In the present monograph I continue the illustration
of the influence of the Non-Aryan East upon Hellas,
a subject which I have discussed in *The Great
Dionysiak Myth*, by the investigation of a particular
Homerik personage and episode. I trust that this
study will bring into still clearer prominence the
fact that the Homerik Poems constitute one of the
earliest, and at the same time most important, links
between the East and the West. The subject is also
in strict continuation of my prior mythological researches; and as I have already treated separately
of the Sun (Dionysos), the Moon (in *The Unicorn: a
Mythological Investigation*), and the Stars (in *The Law
of Kosmic Order*, and *Eridanus: River and Constellation*); so in the myth of Kirkê the two heavenly
protagonists will appear in close connexion, alike with
each other and with the stellar host. As previously
stated, such investigations are intended to be contri-

butions to the new and highly important study of archaic psychology.

The mighty harp of Homer is heptachord; the Poems resolve themselves into a sevenfold aspect, which may be denoted by the terms Religion, Mythology, Folklore, Archaeology, History, Humanity, and Linguistic; and we are very far from the last word upon any of these divisions. Investigators chose this or that branch of Homerik study in accordance with their tastes and opportunities; one works with the spade, another historically at decipherment, a third on the lines of linguistic science, a fourth upon those of comparative mythology. All these labours are truly valuable; the various subjects intertwine and interpenetrate. The goal will be reached, but the end is not yet; and meanwhile we shall do well to recognize the importance of careful and scientific effort in every portion of the field.

Much, not of a strictly linguistic character, still remains to be done in the study of the text of the *Ilias* and *Odysseia*. Especially should all recurring formulas, and epithets either obscure or apparently not particularly appropriate, receive careful attention in a comparative point of view. The unintelligible and the seemingly-unsuitable are constantly survivals from a prior stage, and generally become luminous by the aid of comparison.

The Poems are of course Aryan in character ; the Non-Aryan element, however important, is exceptional and subordinate.

While we reject any imaginary moral grafted on a myth in a comparatively late age, we shall do well at the same time to think of Nature as ' the earliest Gospel of the wise ; ' and of the noblest myths as adumbrating and setting forth, in a certain manner, infinite realities. When Sokratês, in the *Gorgias*, has quoted the Homerik legend of Odysseus in the Shades, and told how the hero saw Minôs, ' holding a sceptre of gold and giving laws to the dead,' he adds these noble and memorable words ;—' Now I am persuaded of the truth of these things, and I consider how I shall present my soul whole and undefiled before the Judge in that day. Renouncing the honours at which the world aims, I desire only to know the Truth, and to live as well as I can, and, when the time comes, to die. And, to the utmost of my power, I exhort all other men to do the same.'

BARTON-UPON-HUMBER :
October 1883.

CONTENTS.

———◦———

ABBREVIATIONS.

Brown, R. Jr., *G. D. M.*—*The Great Dionysiak Myth.* (London : Longmans, 1877–8).

—— *R. M. A.*—*The Religion and Mythology of the Aryans of Northern Europe.* (London : E. Stanford, 1880).

—— *L.*—*Language, and Theories of its Origin.* (London : E. Stanford, 1881).

—— *U.*—*The Unicorn: a Mythological Investigation.* (London : Longmans, 1881).

—— *L. K. O.*—*The Law of Kosmic Order.* (London : Longmans, 1882).

—— *E.*—*Eridanus, River and Constellation.* (London : Longmans, 1883).

Smith, Geo., *C. A. G.*—*Chaldean Account of Genesis,* 2nd edit. By Prof. Sayce.

T.—*Transactions* of the Society of Biblical Archaeology.

THE MYTH OF KIRKÊ:

AN HOMERIK STUDY.

SECTION I.

THE HOMERIK LEGEND OF KIRKÊ.

ODYSSEUS with his ship's crew having escaped from
the Laistrygones, who are described as being giant-
cannibals, comes to the Aiaian Isle, where dwelt
Kirkê, own-sister of Aiêtês and daughter of Hêlios
and Persê daughter of Ôkeanos. On the third day
after their arrival the hero reconnoitres, and having
noticed smoke and flame afar off in the woodland, returns to the ship with a stag upon which the company
feast. Next morning he divides his band, and sends
Eurylochos with 22 men to explore the country.
They find the palace of Kirkê in the forest, surrounded by tame and bewitched wolves and lions.
They hear the goddess singing as she works at a
mighty web; and hail her, and she bids them enter
her gates. Eurylochos alone remains without, and
after long watching returns to Odysseus with the
news that his fellows had disappeared in the palace.

B

Meanwhile, Kirkê having seated her guests, makes them a mess mixed with harmful drugs which cause them to forget their home. When they have drunk the potion she smites them with her magic wand, whereupon they become swine, and are shut up in sties but still retain their human mind. Odysseus now arms himself and sets out to the rescue of his men, and on his way meets with Hermês who instructs him how to behave, and gives him the magic herb *moly*, by means of which he will be enabled to successfully defy the enchantments of Kirkê. Having entered the palace the hero is seated by the goddess on a goodly chair, and given the drugged potion in a golden cup. She smites him with the wand and bids him join his company in the sty, but he is not bewitched and drawing his sword springs upon her. With a great cry she clasps his knees, and surmising that he must be Odysseus, seeks his love. He makes her swear that she will not hurt him when naked, and meanwhile her four handmaids, daughters of the wells, woods and rivers, busy themselves in the halls, and prepare a meal and a bath; one of them washes, anoints with oil and dresses the hero, who, however, refuses to taste the banquet until his comrades are restored to man's estate, which is done accordingly. Odysseus then returns to the the ship and conducts Eurylochos and his fellows to the halls of Kirkê, where they remain in peace and plenty for a year, when the hero's companions suggest to him that it is time to depart; Kirkê consents and informs him that he must seek the Underworld in order to consult the soothsayer Teirêsias, gives him full directions for the perilous journey, and at dawn clothes him, veils her head and passes lightly away, having sent a breeze to fill the vessel's sails. The hero then voyages to the Land of the Dead, and afterwards returns to the abode of Kirkê, who again kindly entertains him and his men and hears his story. Having instructed him respecting several dangers which yet await him, she dismisses him at dawn with a favourable wind.

This brief outline of the Τὰ περὶ Κίρκης will serve to refresh the reader's memory respecting the famous story; and I would also refer him to the excellent *presentation* of the tale by Miss J. E. Harrison,[1] who has very ably illustrated its aspect in poetry and art. She has not, however, thought fit to pass on to the *explication* of the myth, a task which I shall now attempt.[2]

---

[1] *Myths of the Odyssey,* 63 *et seq.*
[2] Where I do not give an original translation of a passage or phrase of the poem, I quote from Butcher and Lang, *The Odyssey of Homer,* 1879.

SECTION II.

KIRKÊ AND KALYPSÔ.

It will facilitate the investigation to compare in the first place the two mysterious goddesses Kirkê and Kalypsô, a process which shows that though the one is not actually a reduplication of the other, yet that they are merely variant phases of the same great power. The principal points of resemblance between them are as follows :—

I. Each is a fair and lovely goddess in a remote island, attended by handmaidens.[1]

II. Each is connected with gold and silver, and weaves a mighty web as she sings.[2]

III. Each is specially described as ' fair-haired.'[3]

IV. Each is specially styled ' an awful goddess of mortal speech.'[4]

V. Each has a beautiful dwelling surrounded by woods.[5]

VI. Each loves the hero who unwillingly returns her passion, and whom she is not permitted to retain.[6]

VII. Each swears solemnly not to injure the hero.[7]

VIII. Each sees that he is bathed and dressed.[8]

---

[1] Cf. *Od.* v. 199; x. 349.
[2] *Ibid.* v. 62; x. 222.
[3] *Ibid.* v. 30; xi. 8.
[4] *Ibid.* x. 136; xii. 449.
[5] *Ibid.* v. x.
[6] Cf. *Ibid.* v. 155; ix. 29–33.
[7] *Ibid.* v. 182–7; x. 345.
[8] *Ibid.* v. 264; x. 364.

IX. Each at dawn ' clad herself in a great shining robe, light of woof and gracious, and about her waist cast a fair golden girdle, and put a veil upon her head.'[1]

X. Each when the hero departed sent a 'welcome breeze' to speed him on his way.[2]

Kalypsô dwells in the isle Ôgygia,[3] ' the navel of the sea ; '[4] but this circumstance implies no necessary difference between the two goddesses, since the name merely means ' ocean,' and so in reality equally applies to any sea-girt island. The names Ôgenos and Ôgên = Ôkeanos,[5] and Ôgenidai = Ôkeanidai.[6] The Norse Oegir (' the Dread '), god of the stormy sea, who reappears in modern times as the well-known *eygre* or tidal river-wave, and the Ogre, are variant phases, originally expressive of the terror excited by the vast and tempestuous sea. So Ôgygês, who appears in Attikê and Boiôtia as an archaic King,[7] is always connected with a flood; and his name is equivalent to ' primeval,' in reference to the supposed pristine watery chaos. M. Lenormant, following Windischmann and Pictet, observes, ' Son nom même paraît dérivé de celui qui désignait primitivement le déluge dans les idiomes aryens, en sanscrit *áugha*.'[8] Pausanias, amongst his almost innumerable valuable

---

[1] *Od.* v. 230-2; x. 545-7. [2] *Ibid.* v. 268; xi. 7 ; xii. 149.
[3] *Ibid.* i. 84.   [4] *Ibid.* 50.   [5] Vide Lykophrôn, 231.
[6] Hesychios, in voc.
[7] Vide Pausanias, I. xxxviii. 7; IX. v. 1 ; Apollonios Rhod. *Argonautika*, iii. 1178.
[8] *Les Origines*, i. 432.

little scraps of obscure mythic pedigree, has preserved the fact that ' the hero Eleusis ' (='the
Coming' Sun-god) was, according to some, the son of
Daeira ('the Knowing') daughter of Okeanos, but
according to others the son of Ôgygês, thus illus-
trating the identity of the two latter. The Sun-god
constantly springs in mythic pedigree from Ocean
and some 'knowing,' *i.e.*, light-bringing, nymph ; for,
primarily, to see=to know, and darkness *is* ignorance
(of the unseen).

The first point of real difference between the two
goddesses is in parentage. Kalypsô is the daughter
of Atlas (' the Enduring '), who ' himself upholds the
tall pillars which keep earth and sky asunder.' [1]
Atlas is a personification of that power which sustains
heaven above earth in kosmic order. The solar
Hêraklês essayed the task, but after a time, *i.e.*, at
night, was feign to retire in favour of the more
enduring Atlas, who thus and also because at night the
(lunar and stellar) heaven, which he upbears, comes
into fullest prominence, is more a nocturnal than a
diurnal personage ; and hence the poet applies to
him the peculiar epithet *oloöphrôn*, a title which he
shares with Aiêtês and Minôs, and which, as Mr.
Gladstone notes, 'seems to imply in some form a
formidable if not injurious craft.' [2] Messrs. Butcher and
Lang render the expression ' wise and terrible,' but I
prefer to translate it by the term ' baleful ;' the ' for-

---

[1] *Od.* i. 52-4 ; cf. *Ibid.* vii. 245.　　　[2] *Juventus Mundi*, 120.

midable craft ' of Atlas and Aiêtês being that of the
nocturnal powers, which finds its expression, amongst
other ways, in the. devices of Kirkê and ' crafty
Kalypsô.' [1]

Kalypsô (' the Coverer '),[2] as the daughter of
Atlas, is a more extended personage than Kirkê ; that
is to say, she=the lunar-and-stellar nocturnal sky.
This light makes cheerful and beautiful the otherwise
' blind cave of night,' in the unseen depth of which
is concealed the melancholy and vanquished Sun, who
mourns for his Dawn-bride. The ' hollow caves ' [3]
of Kalypsô are a prominent feature in her story,
and somewhat strongly contrast with the ' halls '
and ' palace ' of Kirkê ; Kalypsô, too, in another
phase, is more a representative of nature, as Kirkê
is of art. There were caves on the island of Kirkê,[4]
but she did not dwell in them ; Odysseus stored
his goods there. ' The Cave-sun appears again in
the person of Mithra-Mithras ; Porphyry states that,
according to Euboulos, " Zoroaster [Zarathustra]
was the first who consecrated in the mountains of
Persia a cave in honour of Mithra ;" [5] and, again,
" Wherever Mithra was known they propitiated the
god in a cavern." [6] The Mithraik Cave = " The

---

[1] *Od.* vii. 245.

[2] ' *Calypso* was so called because *she hid*—ἐκάλυψε—Ulysses on his
return from Troy ' (Liddell and Scott, in voc.).

[3] *Od.* i. 15 ; v. 57, 155 ; ix. 30. In the latter passage the ' hollow
caves ' of the one goddess are distinctly contrasted with the ' halls ' of
the other.

[4] *Ibid.* x. 424.   [5] *Peri tou en Od. tôn Nymph. Ant.* 2.   [6] *Ibid.* 9.

highly mysterious Cavern "[1] of Kemic [Egyptian] solar mythology.' [2]

The dwelling of Kalypsô is remote in that mysterious sea which towards the West is formed by the undefined blending of the Oversea—the 'mare magnum sine fine,' in which the solar and lunar barques sail; the Ocean-proper, which of unknown and awful vastness enrings the world, the Midgard; and the Undersea, invisible and fathomless to man and in which the golden solar boat-cup disappears. Yet she, like Kirkê, although thus dwelling afar, is peculiarly liable to the sway of Hermês, *i.e.*, the Wind-power upon the clouds, who is able to blot her from heaven and so to destroy in a moment the beauty of her cave. And thus when Hermês is sent to her with a command, it is in his character of Argeiphontês,[3] *i.e.*, he who can put out the thousand starry eyes of Argos ('the Bright'), which orbs Hêrê (the 'Gleaming' heaven) puts in her peacock's tail.[4] Hermês, as the Zeus-messenger, well knows his power; and although the interview between him and Kalypsô is marked by a charming courtesy on both sides, yet when 'the great slayer of Argos' departs, his final word to the goddess is, 'Speed him [Odysseus] now upon his path and have regard unto the wrath of Zeus, lest haply he be angered and bear hard on thee hereafter.' [5]

---

[1] *Litany of Ra*, ap. Naville, *Records of the Past*, viii. 103.
[2] Vide R. B. Jr., *L. K. O.* 64.
[3] *Od.* v. 49.　　　　[4] Vide R. B. Jr., *R. M. A.* sec. iii.; *U.* 76 *et seq.*
[5] *Od.* v. 145–7.

Both Kirkê and Kalypsô are well acquainted with
the awful river Styx [1] ('the Hateful') which was connected with the Undersea,[2] and, being a protagonistic
feature in the realm of death and darkness, became
the very type of the dread Unseen and thus supplied
a concept for the most solemn oaths.

Kalypsô, although upon the whole a more extended ideal than Kirkê, is yet necessarily to a great
extent distinctly lunar, inasmuch as the moon always
is and must be the head of night-light. She is also, as
will further appear, considerably more Aryan in character than her sister goddess. The basis of the
myth is too wide to be monopolised by any special
race of mankind, and therefore some of the stories
connected with it are Aryan in origin whilst others are
not. The former class has been sufficiently referred
to by Aryan mythologists, and Sir G. W. Cox well
says of the dwelling of Kalypsô, that it 'is the home
of Tara Bai, the Star-maiden, of Hindu folklore, the
being who can neither grow old nor die, and the
witchery of whose lulling songs no mortal may with-
stand. It is the Horselberg to which the Venus of
mediæval tradition entices the ill-fated Tanhäuser,
the Ercildoune [the abode of Ursula ('Little-bright-
one,' as opposed to Sol) and her myriad star-maidens]
where the fairy queen keeps Thomas the Rimer a not

---

[1] *Od.* v. 185; x. 514.

[2] Cf. *Od.* x. 509–15 with xi. 21–2. So the Hesiodik Styx is 'the
eldest daughter of Ôkeanos,' and the poet vaguely describes how 'a
branch of ocean flows through black night' (vide *Theogonia,* 775–
806).

unwilling prisoner.'[1]   The majesty, beauty, degradation and horror of the Night-queen are combined in
the varying phases of a single concept—Hekatê, in
her long career from Hesiod to Shakspere.[2]

---

[1] *Introduction to Mythology and Folklore,* 160.

[2] Vide R. B. Jr., *U.* sec. vi. A baseless attempt has been made of
late to identify the Aryan Hekatê with the Kemic frog-headed goddess
Heka, a type of water.   Such errors will always arise from hasty conclusions based upon similarity of sound, and arrived at without due
philological enquiry, or careful analysis of the concepts proposed to be
allied.

SECTION III.

THE IMAGINARY MORAL-LESSON OF THE MYTH.

IT will be desirable in the next place to disentangle from the story a parasitic overgrowth of imaginary morality. This web, which is very different from that of Kirkê, has been chiefly woven around the luckless comrades of Odysseus; and presents a notable instance of the heedlessness with which men form a judgment, and of the facility with which an ancient error is handed down from age to age. Thus we learn that 'Sokrates sees in the beast-form only a symbol of greediness. The Stoics find a sermon ready made to hand : Circe is for them the incarnation of beast-like irrationality. Eustathius discovers in the dread daughter of Helios an impersonation of animal appetite.'[1] Horace becomes quite severely virtuous when he calls his friend's attention to what he supposes were the admirable objects of the 'Trojani belli scriptorem.' Homer,[2] it seems, wrote his poems much for the same moral reasons which induced Johnson to compose *Rasselas*. Intemperance, developed in various ways, produces dismal results at

---

[1] J. E. Harrison, *Myths of the Odyssey*, 89.
[2] I use the name in a covering sense.

Troy; and the bard next proceeds to show 'quid virtus et quid sapientia possit.' He exhibits before us a pattern character—Odysseus, 'proposuit nobis exemplar Ulyssem.' This view is delightfully absurd, and all the more so because it is so gravely and honestly advanced by a wit and worldling like Horace. Odysseus, having very judiciously avoided getting himself killed at Troy, most properly wishes to complete his education by travel; he will make 'the grand tour,' and return to Ithakê vastly improved. 'Multorum providus urbes Et mores hominum inspexit.' After paying a round of visits amongst the Kikones, Lotophagoi, Kyklôpes, Kirkê, Kimmerioi, Shades of the Dead, Seirênes, Skylla, Charybdis, and Kalypsô, he would naturally return home as replete with virtue as Harry Sandford himself. But, alas, even this grand 'exemplar' had no effect upon his infatuated comrades. 'You,' continues Horace to his friend, 'are acquainted with the voices of Sirens and the cups of Circe'—this was no doubt strictly true—'of which if he [Ulysses] had foolishly and greedily drunk with his companions,'—

> 'Sub domina meretrice fuisset turpis et excors,
> Vixisset canis immundus, vel amica luto SUS.' [1]

But suppose some Euemeristic Father of the Church, Clement of Alexandria, Arnobius, Tertullian or Augustine, had said to him, How dare you hold up as an exemplar of virtue a wandering vagabond who

---

[1] *Epist.* I. ii. 1-26.

lived in adultery first with one female and then with another, pretending all the while that he desired nothing so much as to return to his wife? And this story of Circe and Ulysses is most profoundly immoral, not merely in its incidents, but especially in this—that the only sinner of the party was Ulysses himself, who escaped scot-free with many advantages whilst all his unoffending friends were severely punished. To avoid the telling force of arguments such as these when applied to the gods generally, the later Pagan philosophers were feign to take refuge, we may hope in some cases unwillingly, in the tangled jungles of Neo-Platonism where they one and all perished miserably; but had they been Comparative Mythologists, they would have had an easy reply to this objection of their Christian opponents. So from age to age the luckless comrades of the hero have had to bear many a taunt and ' point the moral,' until we reach the *Comus* of Milton and the ' swinish multitude ' of Burke.

But when we turn to the story itself we find no fault stated or implied against the party led by Eurylochos, unless indeed it is a fault to be deceived by superhuman power. There is no suggestion that they drank of the cup ' greedily; ' in the sty they did not enjoy the ' acorns and mast and fruit of the cornel tree, whereon wallowing swine do always batten.' The hero mourns their hapless case ; and a passage, perhaps unexcelled in beauty by any in the whole poem, describes how they were more than restored to

their former estate, not pardoned—for they had done
no wrong.[1]

It is true that ' the hog, as one of the most libidi-
nous of animals, is sacred to Venus ;' and that ' according to the Pythagorean doctrines [based upon a
misconception of this story] lustful men are transformed into hogs.'[2] But there is no suggestion in the
tale that the band of Eurylochos were swinish in any
such sense; nor, again, is any special stress laid upon
their being turned into *swine*, for around the palace
of the goddess were 'bewitched wolves and lions,' and
the fear of Eurylochos was that Kirkê would ' surely
change us all to swine, *or* wolves, *or* lions, to guard
her great house.'[3]

I need not, however, enlarge further upon this
point; for indeed the moment we remember that the
story, whatever its subsequent elements may be, is
based upon the observation of natural phenomena,
which it frequently relates with a truly curious ac-
curacy, we see at once that to seriously predicate
morality or immorality of the personified Sun or his
attendants, of the Moon or of Night, is absurd. From
their long and melancholy degradation in this connexion the gods have been at length set free, and it is
no longer necessary to regard Jupiter, the broad bright
heaven who loves countless nymphs, as the Solomon
of a harem. I am very far from either saying or im-

---

[1] For some good remarks on this subject, vide Rev. W. Lucas Collins,
Homer—the Odyssey, 75 et seq.

[2] Gubernatis, *Zoological Mythology*, ii. 6.   [3] *Od.* x. 432-4.

plying that no profound and moral lessons can be drawn either from the *Odyssey* or from the phenomena of nature; that is altogether another matter. The fact that the Sun is faithless to his bride the Dawn, does not in any way prevent us from drawing from the glorious star the brightest and most ennobling hopes.

SECTION IV.

NEO-PLATONISM ON THE MYTH.

IF at the present day there exists any ancient Euemerist who takes the story of Kirkê and Odysseus to a great extent *au pied de la lettre*, merely stripping off the supernatural element after the fashion in which some sages now treat the Four Gospels, I will not attempt to disturb his repose or

> 'With shadowed hint confuse
> A life that leads melodious days.'

Let him trace in peace the voyage of the hero up the Mediterranean, and in due time bring him back again to Ithakê.　But having got rid of the crude moralist, it is perhaps desirable to notice how his brother in error the Neo-Platonist has dealt with the Kirkê-story. I have noticed[1] that Neo-Platonism was extended and intensified—not of course created—by Christian Euemerism.　Like every other phase of the mind it arises very simply and naturally.　An ancient story, venerable and hallowed, descends to a comparatively late age.　We have long ceased to believe it literally, and yet regard it with affectionate reverence.　It is not truth, but it contains truth.　How?　Marry,

---

[1] *Sup.* Sec. III.

occultly. Are not our apparently simple ancient stories, says Philôn the Jew, in reality as full of profound significance as any of your boasted Hellenik myths treated of by Homer or Hesiod, Sokratês or Platôn? Ay, that they are, as I will show ; nay, more so. New teachings and interpretations were connected with the lives of Abraham and Joseph and others, but the Hellenik world not to be outdone, treated their entire mythology in a similar fashion. The system has but one fault, *i.e.*, it is ‘ founded on unsupported fancy and arbitrary assertion.’ [1] That which with equal facility apparently explains anything and everything, really explains nothing ; just as he who loves every nymph, loves no nymph.

Thus premising, let us hear the Neo-Platonist on the myth. ‘ In the beautiful allegory of Circe,’ says the famous Thomas Taylor, who was every whit as good a Neo Platonist as Olympiodoros the Elder himself, ‘we shall find some deep arcana of philosophy. By the Aeean isle the region of sorrow and lamentation is signified, as is evident from the name of the island itself,’ which he thus connects with αἰαῖ. The reader, who remembers how very comfortably Odysseus and his friends lived there for a year, will naturally pause ere he accepts this etymology. ‘ By Circe we must understand the goddess of sense.’ Fortunately there is no necessity to do so, nor indeed do I know exactly what he means. Feeling that a further explanation was requisite he calls in the aid

---

[1] R. B. Jr., *G. D. M.* i. 67.

of Porphyry, who informs us that 'Homer calls the
period and revolution of regeneration in a *circle,*
Circe [I accept this derivation], the daughter of the
Sun, who perpetually connects and combines all
corruption with generation, and generation again
with corruption;' or, as Miss Harrison puts it more
plainly, 'Porphyry says that Homer has expounded
in the fable of Circe the mystic *cycle* of metempsychosis—life, death, and resurrection; man lives in
human form; he dies and takes the shape of a beast,
whereby he is purified and rises to a higher human
life.'[1]   The idea of an archaic sage—Homer, occultly
setting forth these mysterious truths in a highly
roundabout and involved manner, as a species of
conundrum to exercise the wits of an acute posterity,
is one which need not now be seriously treated.
Moreover both Porphyry and Taylor are far too
enamoured of the phantasy to notice that the poem
itself distinctly negatives any such doctrine.   In the
very next episode of the story—the Nekyia, we have
any amount of evidence of belief that man after death
does *not* 'take the shape of a beast.'   Proklos next
takes up the parable, and announces that 'Circe is
that divine power which moves all the life contained
in the four elements.'   'Her song harmonises the
whole sublunary world.'   Her shuttle is golden,
'because her essence is intellectual, pure, immaterial,
and unmingled with generation.'   Taylor, who is as
good as any of them, continues;—'The companions of

---

[1] *Myths of the Odyssey,* 89.

Ulysses, in consequence of being very imperfect
characters [Poor fellows], are changed into brutes,
i.e., into unworthy and irrational habits and manners.'
Hermes (' Reason ') preserves Ulysses ' who is returning, though slowly '—very slowly, I should say—' to
the proper perfection of his nature.' ' The plant
moly, or temperance, is able to repel the allurements
of pleasure.' [1]   This is exactly what in his case it did
not do.   He had pleasure ; his luckless companions
pain.   Explanations of this character are the ' acorns
and mast ' whereon pseudo-philosophical ' swine do
batten,' but they will not suffice for us and must
stand aside.   ' When it comes to sober investigation
of the processes of mythology, the attempt to
penetrate to the foundation of an old fancy will
scarcely be helped by burying it yet deeper under-
neath a new one.' [2]

[1] *On the Wanderings of Ulysses,* 247–8.
[2] Tylor, *Primitive Culture,* i. 251.

SECTION V.

THE NAME 'KIRKÊ.'

IN the analysis of a mythic concept no point is more important than the meaning of the name of the personage or thing. It is desirable therefore in the next place to determine the signification of the title *Kirkê.*

Souidas explains it thus:—κίρκη. ἢ κιρνῶσα τὰ φάρμακα. ' Sic dicta a miscendis venenis.' This view we may pass by without comment.[1] ἢ παρὰ τὴν κερκίδα. 'Vel ab radio textorio.' This view is far more plausible; *kerkis* is (1) ' the rod or comb by which the threads of the woof were driven home, so as to make the web even and close.'[2] It is also (2) any taper rod, and (3) ' *the prickle* of the electric ray,' besides having other meanings ; and it is further to be noted that *kerkos* = (1) the tail of a beast, and (2) the *phallus*. An archaic title is often replete with meaning and a single explanation frequently by no means exhausts its force. Souidas adds ;—τὰς δὲ παιπαλώσας γυναῖκας Κίρκας φαμέν.[3] 'Feminas autem malarum artium peritas Κίρκας appellamus.'

---

[1] Dr. Hayman, however, adopts it (*The Odyssey of Homer*, ii. 143).
[2] Liddell and Scott, in voc.   [3] In voc. Κίρκη.

Prof. Lauth 'connects the name of *Kirkè* with Colchoi.'[1] This view I reject.

Mr. C. F. Keary, in his interesting *Outlines of Primitive Belief*, has an odd fancy about Kirkê and her sister goddess. He says ;—'Circê and Calypso, I suppose, are the same.' This supposition, as will appear throughout the enquiry, is incorrect. 'Each is very Death herself.'[2] So far as Kalypsô is concerned, let any one read the description of her delightful abode with its charming cheerfulness as related in *Od.* v. and judge for himself. The sweet-voiced beauteous nymph with her golden shuttle, blossoming wood, happy birds, fragrant odours, rich vine-clusters, soft meadows of violets—all formed such a lovely whole, that 'even a deathless god who came there might wonder at the sight and be glad at heart.' 'If Circê's name,' says Mr. Keary, 'do not reveal her nature so nakedly as Calypso's name shows hers, yet we easily recognise by it *death* in one of its many guises—a ravenous animal or bird, a hawk or a wolf. . . κίρκος (whence κίρκη) is given as both hawk and wolf;'[3] and he connects it with a root *krik*, 'to make a grating sound.'

I will not occupy space in showing that almost every line of the story gives a flat contradiction to this fantastic notion, and that Kirkê and Kalypsô killed nobody but were goddesses of life, light and love. But with respect to the meaning of the name

---

[1] Gladstone, *Homeric Synchronism*, 268.
[2] *Outlines of Primitive Belief*, 311.   [3] *Ibid.* 302.

Kirkê, Oppian cir. A.D. 180 calls a kind of wolf *kirkos*, and this is the first time the wolf appears in the connexion, a circumstance which disposes of the notion ; which again is equally disposed of by the fact that the Wolf is not a type of Death but of Darkness,[1] or, by paronomasia (λύκος—λευκός), of light. Kirkê is not a wolf ; she bewitches the wolves,[2] *i.e.*, rules over the subdued dark night. Equally unfortunate is the suggestion about the hawk. *Kirkos* is a hawk as the bird that flies in *circles*, not a word primarily meaning 'hawk ;' and thus the hawk neatly illustrates the real meaning of Kirkê, 'the Circle,' or ' the Circular.' Again, the Hawk is a bird specially sacred to the diurnal Apollôn[3] ; and is quite unconnected with either Night or Death. The bird had the same solar character in Kem. There ' the hawk was sacred to Apollo, whom they call Horus.' [4]

We may therefore agree with Porphyry as to the connexion between *Kirkê* and *kuklos*, whilst dismissing his idea that in *Kirkê* the poet refers to any cycle-of-the-soul. *Kirkos*, a variant form of which is *krikos*, is the Lat. *circus, circulus*, Ang.-Sax. *circul*, from the Aryan root *kar*, to move circularly. The line of thought connected with the rod (*kerkis*) is so supremely appropriate to the concept that it probably supplied a

---

[1] Vide R. B. Jr., *R. M. A.* sec. xii. ; *E.* sec. ix.

[2] *Od.* x. 212.　　　　　　　　[3] *Ibid.* xv. 526.

[4] Aelian, x. 24. Mr. Keary, when replying to Prof. Sayce's criticisms on his work (vide *Academy*, June 6, 1882), says that he 'should never dream' of setting up 'for being a philologist.' Under these circumstances it is rather a pity that he should have ventured on so many novel (and highly questionable) explanations of familiar names.

second meaning to the name which thus = rod + circle ; but the root-idea of the Kirkê-concept being lunar, and also for other reasons, the meaning the ' Round ' or ' Circular ' is undoubtedly the primary signification.[1]

Kerkis, as noticed, means moreover ' the prickle of the electric ray ; ' and this reminds us of a very singular and interesting myth of the death of our hero. Sextus Empiricus, the skeptic sage, who lived in the third century of our era, ' says, in his grumbling way, how can he attach importance to historical tradition when " one man says, for example, that Odysseus died by the hand of his son Telegonos, another that he breathed his last owing to a sea-gull which let fall on his head the sting of a ray-fish." '[2] Miss Harrison gives from a Vase an engraving which probably represents ' Bird letting fall the Trygon [' a kind of *roach* with a prickle in the tail '] on the Head of Odysseus,' or at all events on the head of somebody who, of rather youthful appearance for the hero, is rowing in a boat. The circular fish with long pendant tail is borne in air by a heron. As Miss Harrison notes, the Scholiast on *Od.* xi. 134 has preserved four lines from the *Psychagôgoi* of Aischylos which describe the hero's fate ; and Sophoklês wrote a Play entitled *Odysseus Akanthoplêx* (' the Sting-pierced '), of which some half dozen small fragments are extant.

[1] The mythologist will observe that I pass over phallic considerations as lightly as possible.

[2] Ap. J. E. Harrison, *Myths of the Odyssey*, 112.

Now Têlegonos ' the parricide,' [1] son of Odysseus and Kirkê,[2] whose name describes him as ' the One-born-afar,' *i.e.*, the youthful Sun who makes his appearance in the east [3] from his mysterious birth-place in the Underworld, and who like his sire may not remain with Kirkê, to whose island nevertheless he again returns bringing his father's body,[4] *i.e.*, him-self,[5] slays Odysseus with a spear which he had received from Kirkê, *i.e.*, the Old-sun perishes by the combined power of the Moon and the Young-sun. Teirêsias had prophesied concerning Odysseus ;—' Thine own death shall come upon thee from the sea, a gentle death, which shall end thee foredone with smooth old age.'[6] And this youthful Sun from the sea, a Fish-sun,[7] lets fall his fatal ray upon the bald [8] head of the aged and dying Sun in the western Underworld, who is thus poisoned like Hêraklês and Cheirôn.[9] Therefore when some said that Odysseus died by the hand of Têlegonos, whilst others at-

---

[1] Horace, *Carmina*, III. xxix. 8.   [2] Hesiod, *Theogonia*, 1014.

[3] The realm of Kirkê as the Night-queen is connected with the West as the side of Darkness (Vide R. B. Jr., *E.* sec. xvi.), but for reasons which will subsequently appear, Homerik tradition places the Aiaian island in the East (*Od.* xii. 3, 4; cf. Gladstone, *Homeric Synchronism*, 226 *et seq.*).

[4] Vide Hyginus, *Fabulae*, cxxvii.

[5] As to the ' unconscious blending' of two representations in myths, vide R. B. Jr., *U.* 52.

[6] *Od.* xi. 134–6; xxiii. 281–3.

[7] Vide R. B. Jr., *L. K. O.* secs. xxi. xxiii.

[8] Παλαιὸν δέρμα καὶ τριχορρυές (Aischylos, *Psychagôgoi*, Fragment, ii.).

[9] Vide R. B. Jr., *E.* sec. ix. The considerations in the text do not decide the question whether in addition to a solar hero Odysseus, there was also any historical Odysseus.

tributed his death to the sting of a fish, in truth the same incident was being represented in two variant phases ; and thus the historical contradiction which perplexed Sextus Empiricus is really imaginary. Têlegonos subsequently, naturally enough, married Pênelopê, the Dawn-and-eve-light.

SECTION VI.

AIA, THE ISLAND OF KIRKÊ.

In the Homerik account this mysterious locality [1] is always called ' the Aiaian isle,' [2] or the name appears in the epithet ' Aiaian Kirkê ; ' [3] the name Aia is never used. Now there is a very subtle and curious reason for this, since, if Kirkê be, as we have seen reason

---

[1] It is generally supposed that Aia = Gaia (vide Mayor, *The Narrative of Odysseus*, 139), a short and simple explanation which explains nothing. For how should any place be called ' Land-island,' and especially when it was out at sea? As Mr. Mayor himself notes, following Buttmann, such names as Aiêtês and Mêdeia 'point to an eastern source of these legends;' and if for Aia we should read Gaia, similarly, I presume, for Aiêtês we should read Gaiêtês. Of course every one is aware that Homer often uses αἶα for γαῖα; thus in the account of Kirkê herself we find the expressions πατρίδος αἴης (*Od.* x. 472) and πατρίδα γαῖαν (*Ibid.* 474). But there is no authority for reading γαῖα for αἶα in Herodotos where αἶα is connected with Aiêtês; and in the *Odyssey* itself such passages as *Od.* i. 32 and λ. 135 show that such readings as Αἰαίη and Αἰαίην are not occasioned by any metrical necessity or convenience, as in the above-quoted instances of αἴης and γαῖαν. Dr. Paley in an article (*Pre-Homeric Legends of the Voyage of the Argonauts*) in the *Dublin Review*, explains Aia in the usual way as ' mainland ; ' and says, ' It is to be distinguished from Aeaea.' I think that Kirkê's island also is called Aia, but of course the island is not the place in Kolchis. Dr. Hayman judiciously steers clear of γαῖα, and observes, 'The etymol. of Αἰαίη [The word is an adjective, not a substantive; so Mess. Butcher and Lang ;—' Circe of Aia '] and Αἰήτης [=, according to Dr. Paley, ' King-of-the-mainland '] is doubtful : I incline to connect it with ἠώ-ς the dawn, as if a changed form of ἠωίη ' (*The Odyssey of Homer*, ii. 143). This suggestion is merely the child of despair.

[2] *Od.* x. 135; xii. 3. 　　　 [3] *Ibid.* ix. 31-2 ; xii. 268, 273.

to conclude, the ' Round '-moon, Pandia, ' the full orb which gleams in the nightly sky,'[1] then the island of Aia in which she dwells, must be merely the Moon-island itself, a reduplication of the Moon-goddess, and hence Aiaian=Kirkaian. This then, is the reason of no sharp distinction being drawn between Kirkê and Aia, the place of her abode. The Aiaian isle is there-fore, like Delos, a floating one, now in the east, now in the west; but, as noticed, the Homerik account specially connects it with the former quarter and for this reason:—Kirkê is an eastern personage not merely in general character, a circumstance further illustrated by various special features, but also as the sister of Aiêtês,[2] ' the Baleful ' ('Ολοόφρων).[3] Now Aiêtês, as all antiquity agrees, was king of Kolchis ; and it was from him that the Argonauts stole the Golden-fleece, a story well known to Homer, and it is Kirkê who tells Odysseus when speaking of Skylla and Charybdis, ' One ship only of all that fare by sea hath passed that way, even Argo,[4] that is in all men's minds, on her voyage from Aiêtês.'[5] We have then an ancient name, used in a lunar connexion, and im-pervious to any Aryan etymological explanation ; we must needs therefore, like Iasôn, sail to Kolchis on its quest. Herodotos in his very funny account of the ancient quarrel between the East and the West,[6] thus

---

[1] Sir G. W. Cox, *Mythology of the Aryan Nations,* 2nd edit. p. 372.
[2] *Od.* x. 137. [3] Vide *sup.* Sec. II.
[4] For a full account of the constellation Argô and her voyage, vide R. B. Jr., *E.* sec. v. [5] *Od.* xii. 70.
[6] The Easterns stole Iô; then the Westerns stole Europê, and not

prosaically refers to the Argonauts and their famous vessel ;—' They manned a ship of war, and sailed to Aia, a city of Kolchis, on the river Phasis ; from whence they carried off Mêdeia, the daughter of the king of the land.'[1] Now *Mêdeia*, the niece of Kirkê, and the Aryan signification of whose name is ' the Wise,' the beautiful and dangerous sorceress and poisoner, who at length became immortal and was married to Achilleus in Elysion, is merely a reduplication of her aunt Kirkê ; but, as Sir H. C. Rawlinson long since noted,[2] she, like Andro*medê*,[3] is connected with Media. Aia in the poem of Valerius Flaccus appears as a huntress, like Artemis-Selenê, who was changed into the island of that name in order to protect her from the river Phasis,[4] who followed her as Alpheios pursued Arethousa. This phase of the myth preserves the moving character of the island ;—

' Meek Dian's crest
Floats through the azure skies, an island of the blest.'

Having found the name Aia in Kolchis, we must next explain it. The nationality of the Kolchians is an obscure question ; Herodotos believed them to be an Egyptian colony,[5] but his theory, despite several

satisfied yet, Mêdeia ; in revenge the Easterns stole Helenê ; then the Westerns recovered her and burnt Troy ; then the Easterns under Xerxes burnt Athens. Had Herodotos lived until the time of Alexander he would have been able to have added another link to the chain which indeed has been lengthening ever since his time.

[1] Herod. i. 2 ; cf. Euripides, *Mêdeia*, 2.
[2] Vide Prof. Rawlinson, *Herodotus*, i. 123, note 7.
[3] As to Andromedé, vide R. B. Jr., *U.* 55.
[4] *Argonautica*, i. 742 ; v. 426.   [5] Herod. ii. 104.

interesting resemblances which he traces between the
two nations, must certainly be rejected. Sir H. C.
Rawlinson, having noticed 'the modern theory that
the Colchians were immigrants from India,' a view
which he says is 'not quite satisfactory,' and which
appears to me to be highly dubious, observes ;—'The
Colchians may have been transported from the Persian
Gulf to the mountains of Armenia by some of the
Assyrian monarchs, who certainly transported Chaldaeans to this locality.[1] A people called *Gilkhi* appear
in the extreme north of Armenia, in the inscriptions
of Assyria.' [2] The Kolchians were much darker in
complexion than their neighbours, a circumstance
which Pindar knew prior to Herodotos, as he tells
how the Argonauts fought κελαινώπεσσι Κόλχοισιν
. . . Αἰήτα παρ' αὐτῷ.[3] Prof. Sayce translates a
passage from an Inscription of Tiglath-Pileser I. cir.
B.C. 1150, which speaks of '4000 Kaskayans or
Kolkhians, as soldiers of the Hittites ; '[4] and we see
at once that the Kolchians, whoever they may have
been, were connected in various ways with the
Turanian inhabitants of Western Asia and brought
within the wide sphere of Euphratean and Akkadian
influence.

This view may be further supported by the testimony of Stephanos of Byzantium who, in his *Ethnika*,

[1] In proof of which he cites Moses of Chorênê, ii. 4, 'and the
Armenian Geography, p. 356, where Chaldaeans are mentioned among
the Colchians.'
[2] Rawlinson, *Herodotus*, iv. 185.   [3] *Pyth.* iv. 376–80.
[4] *T.* vii. 298.

under the heading Χαλδαῖοι, says, Εἰσὶ δὲ Χαλδαῖοι ἔθνος πλησίον Κολχίδος. In support of this he quotes a line from the *Tympanistai* of Sophoklês :—

Κόλχος τε Χαλδαῖός τε καὶ Σύρων ἔθνος.

Sir H. C. Rawlinson, when noticing the myth of Iô, remarks that ' as the wanderings of Io have been often compared with the erratic course of the moon in the heavens, passing in succession through all the signs of the zodiac, so do we find . . . the primitive Chaldaean title [of the moon] represented by a Cuneiform sign, which is phonetically AI, as in modern Turkish.'[1] So Strahlenberg in his ' Polyglot-Table of the Dialects of 32 Tartarian Nations,' gives as moon-names :—Siberian-Mahometan-Tartars, AY ; Jakuti on the river Lena, UICH ; Ostiaks, IRE ; Ostiaks near Tomskoi, IRRAED ; Samojedi-Tawgi, IRI.[2] M. Lenormant, when noticing Akkadian and Altaic affinities, gives ;—' Moon. Accad., As. Turk., and Osmanli, AI.'[3] Mr. Gerald Massey, in his ' Comparative Vocabulary of Akkado-Assyrian and Egyptian Words,' which he states has been ' severely taxed, queried and abbreviated by Mr. Theo. G. Pinches,' the well-known Assyriologist, compares Ak. *aa*, ' moon,' ' father,' with the Kemic *aah*, ' moon.'[4] M. Lenormant gives ' *a*, subst. " père." Abrégé du plus habituel et plus complet AI.'[5] Now we had arrived from totally different

---

[1] Rawlinson, *Herodotus*, i. 123.
[2] *Description of Siberia*, 1738.   [3] *Chaldean Magic*, 304.
[4] *A Book of the Beginnings*, ii. 443.
[5] *Étude sur quelques parties des Syllabaires Cunéiformes*, 277.

considerations at the conclusion that AIA must be simply the Moon. Ethnology and philology here step in and certify the fact, and I think that this result, arrived at by two independent lines of research, must be regarded as a demonstration. But further: the remarkable Homerik description of Kirkê states that she is

Αὐτοκασιγνήτη ὀλοόφρονος Αἰήταο.[1]

Who, then, is Aiêtês the Kolchian, son of the Sun, and from whom the heroes in their solar barque steal and bring westward the golden solar fleece, Aries?[2] The Night-king, the Male-moon, Lunus, whose 'own-sister' and other self is Luna. He is the great Akkadian Zu-en (the 'Wise-lord,' Oloüphrôn in the good sense in non-Hellenik regions), the Assyrian Sin; and *en* also signifies 'lip,' *i.e.*, incantation,[3] which exactly suits his character and the natures of Kirkê and Mêdeia. We can therefore well understand the statement that he was driven from his kingdom by his brother Persês[4] (the Sungod), but restored to it again by his daughter Mêdeia[5] (the lunar power), a reduplication of himself. For

---

[1] *Od.* x. 137.   [2] Vide R. B. Jr., *L. K. O.* sec. x.   Aries, the Ram.
[3] Sayce, *Assyrian Grammar*, Syl. No. 514.   Cf. *e* (No. 239), 'to speak,' all speech having been at first regarded as semi-magical.
[4] 'Persê is the wife of Hêlios; the Titan Persês is husband of Asteria ("the Starry-heaven"); Perseus is the solar hero, son of Zeus in the form of a gleaming golden shower, and his son Persês is the mythic sire of the Persians. . . The name is connected with heavenly and solar brightness and splendour' (R. B. Jr., *G. D. M.* i. 279. For further consideration of Perseus, vide R. B. Jr., *U.* 51 *et seq.*; 91).
[5] Apollodôros, I. ix. 28.

this contest of the hostile brethren is the ancient
battle between the Twins (Gemini),[1] Sun and Moon,
who, in the curious version of the story preserved
by Nicolas of Damaskos,[2] are called Parsondas and
Nannaros.   This latter name is the Assyrian Nannaru
('the Brilliant'), a name of the Moon-god.[3] In Sondas
M. Lenormant finds a variant of Sandan, a sun-god
whose cult was widely spread in Asia Minor. 'The
Ak. *sam*, As. *samsu*, is "the sun," and the Ak. *dan*, As.
dannu, "strong." Sandan is the equivalent of Raman,
the Aquarius-sun and Meridian-sun.'[4] *Par* is an
Akkadian name of the sun.[5] Parsondas therefore
probably = Sun + Strong-sun (intensive).   As Parsa
(Persia, from *pars*, 'a horseman,' the modern Persian
and Arabic Fars) in Greek becomes Persis, and Persês
son of Perseus and Andromedê was, according to the
Hellenes, the eponymous sire of the Persians, we see
at once how close is the connexion between Persês
and Pars-ondas. Not that I would in any way confuse
the Ak. *par* with the Old Pers. *pars*, but that the
instance shows that the form *pars* would probably reappear in Gk. as Persês.   Parthenios (tem. Augustus)
in his *Peri Erôtikôn Pathêmatôn*, says that Assaôn was
the father of Niobê, and Prof. Sayce observes, 'It is
possible that Sandan or Sandôn may lie concealed in
Assaôn.'[6]

[1] Vide R. B. Jr., *L. K. O.* sec. xii.
[2] *Fragment*, x.   [3] Vide Lenormant, *Les Origines*, i. 161, note 7.
[4] R. B. Jr., *E.* 80.
[5] Vide Sayce, *Assyrian Grammar*, Syl. No. 402.
[6] *Academy*, July 28, 1883.

Amongst other Akkadian moon-names is Idu ('the Measuring-lord'[1]), and the word is the equivalent of the As. *arkhu*, Heb. *yerakh*, 'month,' the moon being as of course the month-measurer.[2] This name has been fortunately preserved in a Greek form by Hesychios, who gives Ἀϊδὼ, Ἀϊδῆς· ἡ σελήνη παρὰ Χαλδαίοις. A variant of Idu is ITU.[3] Now as Idu = (Gk.) Aïdês, so Itu = Aïtês. But as Ai is the Moon, and Aia the Moon-island, we obtain the form Aiaïtês = Aiïtês = Aiêtês = AIITU ('the Moon-the-measuring-lord'). Truly is Ai 'own-sister' to Aiïtu.

Prof. Sayçe, after recently observing that 'in early Accadian mythology the mouth of the Euphrates was identified with the river of death,' adds, 'The Okeanos of Homer had, I believe, its origin in this Accadian river, which coiled itself round the world.'[4] The Homerik Kimmerioi, again, whose 'land and city' was at 'the limits of the world . . . shrouded in mist and cloud,'[5] hard by Ôkeanos, reappear in the cuneiform Inscriptions as the Gimirraai, 'with whom Esarhaddon fought in the north-east of Assyria;'[6] and of whom Assurbanipal speaks as the 'wasters of the people of the country' of 'Guggu (Gyges) King of Luddi'[7] (Lydia). Prof. Sayce also

---

[1] From *id*, a measure, + *U*, lord.   [2] Vide R. B. Jr., *U.* 33.
[3] Sayce, *Assyrian Grammar*, Syl. No. 110.
[4] Vide R. B. Jr., *E.*, Introduction, x.   [5] *Od.* xi. 14–15.
[6] *T.* iv. 292.
[7] Vide Geo. Smith, *Assyrian Discoveries*, 331–2. So Aischylos 'places Cimmeria (*Prométheus Desmôtês*, 748–50) in close proximity to the Palus Maeotis and the Bosphorus' (Rawlinson, *Herodotus*, iii. 151; cf. *Herod.* iv. 12).

seems to agree that Mr. Gladstone[1] is 'right in seeing in the Κήτειοι of Homer[2] the Hittites of Carchemish.'[3] I mention these circumstances as a few instances of traces left in the Homerik Poems of knowledge of the remoter localities of Western Asia, so that it may at once appear that there is nothing *primâ facie* surprising in the fact that Homer should have preserved an archaic Euphratean sacred name. Indeed I doubt not but that it will ultimately be proved that Euphratean influence was a very distinct, although of course a subordinate, factor in the component elements of the Poems.

The foregoing considerations suggest the question, Have we here any fresh data to apply to the enquiry respecting the time when such a line as that above quoted, and which describes the relationship between Kirkê and Aiêtês and his character, was composed? Every one knows that the Homerik Poems, whatever may be the date of their reduction into a form practically the same as that in which we have them, are replete with ideas highly archaic ; and if we detect in them an Akkadian substratum in parts, this fact is thereby intensified. But what could the poet have known of the obscure and peculiar points of which he treats with such clearness, precision and consistency, except by traditions which even then must have been very ancient? No one, I presume, would assert that his employment of the special term

---

[1] *Homeric Synchronism,* 170 *et seq.*   [2] *Od.* xi. 521.
[3] *T.* vii. 254.

oloöphrôn (which in the *Ilias* is only used of a
serpent,[1] a lion,[2] and a boár [3]) as the characteristic
epithet of the three mysterious personages Atlas,
Aiêtês and Minôs,[4] is either arbitrary or accidental.
It is an epithet of double aspect, denoting at once
superiority of some kind, and that superiority exercised to the hurt of others; the name is good or
bad according to the standpoint of the individual,
whether *e.g.* he reveres or simply dreads Aiêtês.
The view that Kirkê was 'own-sister' of the latter
must have been equally archaic, for the poet certainly had not Lunus and Luna in his mind. For
centuries, then, ere his day men had spoken of
'Kirkê own-sister of baleful Aiêtês;' and as it is
clear that he did not invent these statements, so it is
very doubtful whether he gave them their present
form; that is to say, such a verse (it consists of but
three words) containing two then purely traditional
and unintelligible statements, was probably a quotation from the earlier time, and merely repeated by
the poet whoever he was and whenever he may have
lived.

[1] *Il.* ii. 723.   [2] *Ibid.* xv. 630.   [3] *Ibid.* xvii. 21.   [4] *Od.* xi. 322.

SECTION VII.

SOME NON-HOMERIK NOTICES OF KIRKÊ.

ERE further considering the Homerik story let us
notice a few non-Homerik references to the 'fair
goddess;' for these also may be of great antiquity
and importance, and we shall be able to contrast
them with Homerik detail and to see how far the
whole agrees. Hesiod (as we have him) says;—
'Kirkê, daughter of Hêlios son-of-Hyperîôn, by the
love of Odysseus of-enduring-heart bare Agrios and
Latînos blameless and strong. Têlegonos too she bare
through golden Aphroditê.'[1] Of Agrios, otherwise
Argios, nothing is known 'and in all probability the
name is corrupt.'[2] Latînos, so markedly praised, we
may dismiss; as Prof. Mahaffy observes, 'Some parts
of the conclusion [of the Theogony] have been
tampered with, especially where Latinus and the
Tyrrhenians are mentioned, for though Strabo holds
that Hesiod knew Sicily, . . . it is absurd to foist
upon him any statement about the descent of Latinus
from Ithacan parentage.'[3] The line respecting Têlegonos is almost certainly spurious. The residuum is

---

[1] *Theogonia,* 1011–14.　　　[2] Paley, *Hesiod,* 251.
[3] *History of Classical Greek Literature,* i. 111–12.

that Kirkê, as in the Homerik account, is Ἡελίου θυγάτηρ, and that she became by Odysseus the mother of somebody. Hêlios is the son of Hyperîôn, as in Homer;[1] that is to say, the Meridian-sun is son of the ' Climbing '-sun of early morning.

' Apollonius Rhodius, when he revived the epic form, recreated Circe with something of her old godhead, as mistress, however, of the rights of purification, as the stern rebuker of sin.'[2] This is altogether removed from the Homerik presentation. ' Circé voulant purifier Médée et Jason du meurtre d'Absyrthe, étendit d'abord sur l'autel un jeune porceau, et l'ayant égorgé, elle teignit de son sang les mains des deux coupables.'[3]

On the chest of Kypselos, Kirkê and Odysseus were represented asleep, whilst the four Homerik attendants of the goddess were depicted fulfilling the offices assigned to them in the poem.[4]

Nonnos makes Kirkê the mother of Phaunos (Faunus) by Zeus;[5] and calls her 'rock-loving' (φιλοσκόπελος),[6] possibly in allusion to the σκοπιὴν παιπαλόεσσαν[7] on her island. He also refers to the φάρμακα ποικίλα Κίρκης,[8] the Homerik φάρμακα λύγρα.[9]

Strabo mentions that the tomb of Kirkê was

[1] *Od.* xii. 176.
[2] J. E. Harrison, *Myths of the Odyssey,* 89; vide *Argonautika,* iv. 666–715.
[3] Rolle, *Culte de Bacchus,* i. 42; vide Apollodoros, I. ix. 24.
[4] Pausanias, V. xix. 7.   [5] *Dionysiaka,* xiii. 330.
[6] *Ibid.* xxxvii. 56.   [7] *Od.* x. 194.   [8] *Dionysiaka,* xxxvii. 418.
[9] *Od.* iv. 230; x. 236.

shown on the larger of the two small islands called
Pharmakoussai ('fit name for the last abode of a
"Pharmakeutria"'[1] — Sorceress) in the bay of
Eleusis.[2] The island is now named Megali Kyra.
Strabo has also a good deal to say about the goddess
in his introductory remarks on Homer, but his observations are of no special value. Thus he shows
by Homerik quotations that Kirkê somewhat ex-
aggerated the future perils of Odysseus;[3] and notes
that Aithalia (Elba) had a harbour named after the
Argô, 'Iasôn having sailed hither, seeking the abode
of Kirkê, as Mêdeia wished to see that goddess.'[4]
He says, 'They say' that Mount Circaeum, off the
coast of Latium, 'contains numerous roots, but this
perhaps is only to harmonize with the myth of
Kirkê.' 'A temple of Kirkê stood there,' and 'a
cup is shown which belonged to Odysseus,'[5] a truly
interesting relic. The Latin poets, who carefully
applied the voyage of Odysseus as far as possible
to the actual geography of the Western Mediterranean, have also deposited the goddess on this spot.
Thus Vergil sings of Aeneas and his comrades :—

'Proxima Circaeae raduntur litora terrae,
Dives inaccessos ubi Solis filia lucos
Assiduo resonat cantu, tectisque superbis
Urit odoratam nocturna in lumina cedrum,
Arguto tenues percurrens pectine telas.
Hinc exaudiri gemitus, iraeque leonum
Vincla recusantum et serâ sub nocte rudentum :

[1] Mayor, *The Narrative of Odysseus*, 139.
[2] Strabo, IX. i. 13.   [3] Ibid. I. ii. 36.
[4] Ibid. V. ii. 6.   [5] Ibid. V. iii. 6.

Setigerique sues, atque in praesepibus ursi
Saevire, ac formae magnorum ululare luporum :
Quos hominum ex facie Dea saeva potentibus herbis
Induerat Circe in vultus ac terga ferarum.' [1]

The Circaean promontory (Monte Circello)—' once
an island ' [2]—was famous also for a kind of marble
much used by the Etruscans.[3] Strabo further says ;—
' The city of Aia, close by the Phasis, is still pointed
out. Aiêtês is generally believed to have reigned in
Colchis ; *the name is still common throughout the
country*, and tales of the sorceress Mêdeia are yet
abroad.' [4] We should of course naturally expect that
the name of the lunar divinity would impress itself
upon local nomenclature, just as in the Euphrates
Valley we find Ur (' Light,' *i.e.*, Moon) ' the capital
of the earliest Accadian dynasty with which we are
acquainted. It was specially devoted to the worship
of the moon-god, the ruins of whose temple have
been discovered there.' [5] The Moon-god as the
' Lord of Ur ' is thus addressed in an Akkadian
Hymn :—

' Lord ! prince of gods of heaven and earth, whose mandate is
　　exalted !
　Father ! god enlightening earth ! Lord ! good god, of gods the
　　prince !
　Timely crescent, mightily horned, doom-dealer splendid with orb
　　fulfilled !
　Self-produced, from his home forth issuing, pouring evermore
　　plenteous streams !

---

[1] *Aeneid*, vii. 10–20.
[2] Mayor, *The Narrative of Odysseus*, 138.   Vide authorities cited.
[3] Vide Dennis, *Cities and Cemeteries of Etruria*, edit. 1878, i. 246 etc.
[4] Strabo, I. ii. 39.　　　　　　　　[5] *C. A. G.* 318.

High-exalted, all-producing, life unfolding from above!
Primeval seer, rewarder sole, fixing the doom of days remote!
Unshaken chief, whose hand benign is never mindful of thy
    wrongs,
Whose blessings cease not, ever flowing; leading on his fellow-
    gods,
Who from depth to height bright-piercing openeth the gate of
    heaven.
Lord whose power benign extendeth over all the heaven and
    earth!
Who in heaven is high-exalted? Thou! Sublime is thy behest!
Thou thy will in heaven revealest. Thee celestial spirits praise!
Thou! Thy will in heaven as the luminous ether shines!
Lord! in heaven and earth none equals thee.' [1]

Such, then, is Aiêtês Oloöphrôn in his home.
The name Sennacherib (Sin-akhi-irib) supplies a fami-
liar instance of the introduction of the title of the
Moon-god (Sin) into the designation of an historical
Euphratean personage.[2]

In two other passages [3] Strabo introduces Kirkê,
and professes to be able to discriminate between
actual facts recorded by 'Homer' and the poet's
plausible inventions. But when we find that he
places amongst the former the voyage of the Argô
and amongst the latter the relationship of Aiêtês,
Kirkê and Mêdeia, even quoting the famous line
Od. x. 137,[4] we see at once that his remarks merit
no special attention.

The notices of the goddess in Hyginus,[5] Souidas,[6]
and Porphyry [7] have been already cited.

---

[1] Ap. Lenormant (Vide *Journal of the Transactions of the Victoria
Institute,* xii. 115).

[2] Cf. the Kemic Aahmes (Amasis), 'Moon-born.'

[3] Strabo, I. ii. 10, 40.   [4] *Sup.* Sec. VI.   [5] *Sup.* Sec. V.

[6] *Sup.* Ibid.   [7] *Sup.* Secs. IV., V.

Ovid relates how Circe through love of Glaucus transforms the nymph Scylla into a hideous monster.[1] The poet informs us that ;—

> ' Scylla loco mansit, quumque est data copia primum,
> In Circes odium sociis spoliavit Ulixen.'

Vergil says ;—

> ' Carmina vel caelo possunt deducere Lunam:
> Carminibus Circe socios mutavit Ulyssei ; '[2]

thus coupling Luna and Circe. Elsewhere he alludes to the fate of Picus[3] whom Circe was said to have changed into a woodpecker. He also charges ' Daedala Circe ' with having stolen horses from her sire.[4] This epithet connects the goddess with oriental regions. ' It is Daidalos (" the Cunning-worker "), the personification of the statuary's craft, who in Phoenicia, Krêtê, and then subsequently westward, introduces a development of art hitherto unknown. He, according to tradition, first wrought his figures with separate feet, and so was credited with having, Hêphaistos-like, made living statues.'[5]

Horace thinks that a song ' on the Teian lyre ' about ' Laborantes in uno Penelopen vitreamque Circen,'[6] is pleasant in the shade on a hot day. He also alludes to ' Tusculi Circaea moenia,'[7] the city

---

[1] *Metam.* xiv. 1 *et seq.*   [2] *Ecloga,* viii. 69–70.
[3] *Aeneid,* vii. 189–91.   [4] *Ibid.* 282–3.
[5] R. B. Jr., *G. D. M.* i. 355; cf. Pausanias, IX. iii. 2, 3; Themistios, *Orat.* xv.; Palaiphatos, *Peri Apistôn.* According to Homer (*Il.* xviii. 592) Daidalos made a *choros* or circular dancing-place for Ariadnê.
[6] *Carmina,* I. xvii. 19–20.   [7] *Epodon,* I. 29–30.

being reputed to have been founded by Têlegonos.[1] A further reference of his to the goddess I have already noticed.[2]

The Homerik Hymn *Kaminos* ('The Furnace') contains the invocation :—

Δεῦρο καὶ Ἡελίου θύγατερ, πολυφάρμακε Κίρκη,
Ἄγρια φάρμακα βάλλε, κάκου δ' αὐτούς τε καὶ ἔργα.[3]

The word *agria*, Lat. *dira*, perhaps explains the mysterious Agrios whom, as above noticed, Hesiod gives to the goddess as a son.

'In the *Orlando Innamorato*, when the Count views the story of "Ulysses and Circella" depicted on a "fair arcade," judgment has fallen upon the enchantress' who is herself 'turned to a milk-white hart.'[4]

The Author or Authors of 1 *Henry VI.* allude to our goddess. York says of La Pucelle ;—

'See, how the ugly witch doth bend her brows,
As if, with Circe, she would change my shape.'[5]

In Milton's delicious poem, Comus is the son of Bacchus and Circe. Mr. R. C. Browne observes, 'Warton quotes [apropos of *Comus*] Plutarch's dialogue of Gryllus, wherein some of the victims of Circe, disgusted with the vices and vanities of human life, refused to be re-transformed.'[6]

Noël says of Kirkê, 'Magicienne habile, au point

---

[1] Vide *Carmina*, III. xxix. 8.   [2] *Sup.* Sec. III.   [3] Vs. 15-16.
[4] J. E. Harrison, *Myths of the Odyssey*, 87.
[5] Act v. Scene iii.   [6] *Comus* (Clarendon Press Series), 38.

de faire descendre les étoiles du ciel, elle ne l'était pas
moins dans l'art des empoisonnements. Le premier
essai qu'elle fit de ses talents en ce genre, fut sur le roi
des Sarmates, son mari ; crime qui la rendit si odieuse
à ses sujets, qu'ils la forcèrent à prendre la fuite. Le
Soleil la transporta dans son char,[1] sur la côte de
l'Etrurie, nommée depuis le Cap de Circé, et l'île
d'Ea devint le lieu de sa résidence.'[2] This is mainly
based on the account in Diodoros who says, as quaintly
' made English by G. Booth,' 1718, that Hekatê ' was
the first that found out *Aconitum*.[3] . . She Marry'd
Æetes, and had by him Two Daughters Circes [Kirkê]
and Medea. Circes likewise being much addicted to
the Compounding of all sorts of Medicines, found out
the wonderful Natures and efficacy of divers sorts of
Roots and Herbs, many she learnt of her mother
Hecate, but many more she discovered by her own
industry. . . This Circes was Marry'd to the King
of the Sarmatians (Σαρματῶν), whom some call
Scythians ; but she likewise poyson'd her Husband,
and so usurping the Kingdom, executed many
Butcheries and Cruelties upon the Subjects ; for
which (as some Writers relate) she was driven out of
her Kingdom, and fled to the Ocean (φυγεῖν ἐπὶ τὸν
ὠκεανόν), and possessing herself of a certain Desert
Island, settl'd there, together with the Women her
Companions. But as other Historians say, leaving

---

[1] Apollonios Rhod. iii. 310.

[2] *Dictionnaire de la Fable,* 1810, in voc. *Circé.* This work is a valuable compilation.

[3] She would seem to have been an archaic homoeopathist.

Pontus (ἐκλιποῦσαν τὸν Πόντον), she settl'd in the Promontory of Italy, now called from her Circeum.'[1] Diodoros, notwithstanding the intense crassness of his Euemerism,[2] is often very valuable; inasmuch as having before him many important works now lost, he has preserved numerous highly interesting and significant facts, of the meaning of which he was wholly ignorant. Here we notice several very important points respecting the goddess. (1) She is connected with Kolchis, and Sarmatia Asiatica north of Kolchis; (2) is at once, as this account in full shows, highly amorous and cruel; (3) proves fatal to her eastern husband; and (4) flies westward to the ocean.[3]

In Art—vases, gems, mirrors, lamps, wall-paintings, sarcophagoi, etc., we find numerous representations of the Kirkê-myth; *e.g.*, Kirkê mixing the magic cup, enchanting a Comrade of Odysseus, with Odysseus, feeding a Hog, imploring mercy of Odysseus, with Odysseus and Mentôr, giving her commands to Têlegonos, and at the burial of Odysseus by Têlegonos.

---

[1] Diodoros, iv. 45.

[2] *E.g.* he is content to dispose of Hellê in the myth thus:—'Helles by leaning too much forward over the sides of the Ship to vomit, fell overboard into the Sea' (Booth's Translation).

[3] Cf. a charming modern poet:—

'Cry to the moon to sink her lingering horn In the dim seas, and let the day be born.'

SECTION VIII.

THE MYTHIC RELATIVES OF KIRKÊ.

THE Homerik pedigree of the goddess and her brother Aiêtês is as follows ;—' Both were begotten by Êelios, who gives light to all men, and their mother was Persê, daughter of Ôkeanos.'[1] According to the formal, parish-register-like account of Apollodôros, Aiêtês, Kirkê, and Pasiphaê the wife of Minôs, were the children of Hêlios and Persêis[2] (= Persê). He adds that the four sons of Phrixos by Chalkiopê daughter of Aiêtês were Argos ('White'), Melas (' Black '), Phrontis (' Thought '), and Kytisôros, a name not admitting of any Aryan explanation, and recalling the Akkadian Kisar (Lower-expanse) and Sar (Upper-expanse), which reappear as the Kissarê and Assôros of Damaskios.[3] By Chalkiopê, wife of ' the frigid Phrixos,'[4] I understand the Copper-moon, a variant phase of her sire. As to Pasiphaê (' the All-gleaming ') the starlit-heavens, ' when Hêlios sinks to the Underworld, then his daughter Pasiphaê becomes apparent in the silvery skies of night illu-

---

[1] *Od.* x. 138–9. [2] *Bibliothêkê*, I. ix. 1. [3] *Peri Archôn*, cxxv.

[4] Sir G. W. Cox, *Mythology of the Aryan Nations*, 448. Phrixos is the cold, unsunlit air; ' the name is connected with our *freeze* ' (*Ibid.* 384, note).

mined by the countless Argos-eyes.'[1] Pasiphaê is of course the sister of the Moon, and Kirkê + Pasiphaê = Kalypsô.

Cotta, in Cicero's famous dialogue, asks, 'Shall Ino, whom the Greeks call Leucothea, and we Matuta, be reputed a goddess, because she was the daughter of Cadmus, and shall that title be refused to Circe and Pasiphae, who had the Sun for their father, and Perseis, daughter of the Ocean, for their mother? It is true Circe has divine honours paid her by our colony of Circaeum; therefore you call her a goddess; but what will you say of Medea, the granddaughter of the Sun and the Ocean, and daughter of Aetes and Idyia?'[2]

Hesiod says, 'To Hêlios the unwearied the renowned daughter-of-Ôkeanos, Persêis bare both Kirkê and Aiêtês the king. And Aiêtês son of mortal-lighting Hêlios by the will of the gods wedded a daughter of Okeanos, final ($\tau\epsilon\lambda\acute{\eta}\epsilon\nu\tau o\varsigma$) stream [*i.e.*, since all others flow into it], fair-cheeked Idyia.'[3] Like Homer he does not mention Pasiphaê, but the view which made her one of the family is both ancient and wide-spread, as well as being correct in itself. Thus Pausanias, too, not to mention others, calls Hêlios ' the father of Pasiphaê.'[4]

Arnobius, enumerating Euemeristically the various Suns in heathen mythology, says;—' The fifth is regarded as the son of a Scythian king and subtle

---

[1] R. B. Jr., *G. D. M.* ii. 142. [2] *De Naturâ Deorum*, iii. 19.
[3] *Theogonia*, 956–60. [4] *Periêgêsis*, V. xxv. 5.

Circe,'[1] a brief but valuable reference to the goddess. In the late poem the *Argonautika*, which has been included amongst the *Orphika*, Kirkê is called a daughter of Hyperîon[2] (= Hêlios). As noticed,[3] she is the mother of Têlegonos. The above account is both perfectly simple and harmonious. Persê-Persêis is the female phase of Persês the Sun-god ;[4] and I may observe that double sex is frequently attributed by the Akkadians to the heavenly bodies. Thus on a famous uranographic Babylonian Stone which I have elsewhere carefully examined, the Sun is shown ' in variant duplicate as male and female.'[5] And thus we read of the planet Venus :—

' Venus is a female at sunset.
Venus is a male [6] at sunrise.
Venus at sunrise (is) the Sun-god ; thus a male.
Venus at sunset (is) the god Adar ; thus an androgyne.
Venus at sunrise (is) Istar [and thus a female] by name.'[7]

Persê is the daughter of Ôkeanos [8] because Hêlios springs

---

[1] *Adversus Gentes*, iv. 14.　　[2] V. 1221.　　[3] *Sup.* Sec. VI.
[4] Vide *Sup.* Sec. VI.　　[5] Vide R. B. Jr., *E.* 58.
[6] ' The Assyrian word here is very remarkable, *zi-ca-rat*, as if we could coin a term like male-ess. It translates the Accadian " male-female"' (Prof. Sayce).
[7] Prof. Sayce, in *T.* iii. 197.
[8] Dr. Hayman, whose learning and labours in the Homerik question merit deep respect, entertains some singular opinions on various mythological points. Thus, apropos of Persê, he observes, ' To be daughter of Oceanus stands for remoteness from all known connexions, and seems to show that the Greeks had forgotten the ancient cradle of their race in the Aryan highlands' (*The Odyssey of Homer*, ii. 143). As in *Il.* xiv. 201, Ôkeanos is styled ' father of the gods' (A. Lang), or ' source of

Ἐξ ἀκαλαρρείταο βαθυρρόου Ὠκεανοῖο.[1]

As in Kemic (Egyptian) mythology the Scorpion of Darkness is 'the Daughter [*i.e.* Successor] of the Sun,[2] so is the lunar Kirkê the daughter of Hêlios; of whom again she is equally the mother, as shown by the interesting mythic legend preserved by Arnobius. The daughter of Hêlios easily becomes the mother of Têlegonos; and her husband, 'the Scythian king,' is 'the King of the Sarmatians, whom some call Scythians,' who, as noticed,[3] is mentioned by Diodoros. The associations of Sun and Moon are alike eastern and western, but those of Hêlios, Kirkê and Aiêtês have a strong additional eastern character arising from an actual historical cult.[4] In the poems, as Mr. Gladstone observes, 'Helios is marked as an

deities' (Gladstone), it would seem that the whole heavenly hierarchy were as 'remote' as the lovely goddess of any ocean-buried isle. How such a simile shows that 'the Greeks had forgotten the cradle of their race,' I know not. The real explanation, as given in the text, is simplicity itself. But in truth Dr. Hayman's standpoint on such matters is essentially insufficient, inasmuch as it does not recognize the just claims of the Natural Phenomena Theory. Thus, to take another instance, he has a long note about Atlas and his 'pillars' (vide *sup.* Sec. II.) and says in conclusion, 'I believe, with Hermann, that he personifies the spirit of adventurous exploration and the experience which it confers. He "knows the depths of all the sea," and at the same time consistently "holds the pillars" which mark the limits of that knowledge' (*The Odyssey of Homer*, ii. cxi.). The adventurous explorer of Homerik times certainly did *not* know 'the depth of all the sea,' nor could he possibly 'hold' 'the tall pillars which keep earth and sky asunder.' Such explanations irresistibly remind us of Lord Bacon and the Sphinx.

[1] *Il.* vii. 422; *Od.* xix. 434. The conplet of which the above forms the second line appears in both poems and was evidently an ancient and 'well-accustomed' expression.

[2] *Funereal Ritual*, lxxxvi.; vide R. B. Jr., *L. K. O.* sec. xvii.

[3] *Sup.* Sec. VII.　　　　[4] Cf. *Sup.* Sec. VI.

Eastern god;'[1] and the poet naturally connects his children with the same bright quarter. All the historical traditions, too, respecting Aiêtês would place him somewhere in the far East; thus Mimnermos cir. B.C. 630 sings of

Αἰήταο πόλιν, τόθι τ' ὠκέος Ἠελίοιο
ἀκτῖνες χρυσέῳ κείαται ἐν θαλάμῳ,
Ὠκεανοῦ παρὰ χεῖλος, ἵν' ᾤχετο θεῖος Ἰήσων.[2]

Therefore the poet who certainly did not regard Kirkê as being simply Lunà, had every reason to speak of Aia as ' the dwelling place of early Dawn and her dancing grounds,'[3] and the land of sunrising.'[4]

As the combined Aiêtês-Kirkê represents an androgynous moon, *i.e.*, the ascription of both male and female potentialities to the lunar power; so we find that the Egyptians μητέρα τὴν Σελήνην τοῦ κόσμου καλοῦσι, καὶ φύσιν ἔχειν ἀρσενόθηλυν οἴονται;[5] a fact confirmed by the late writer called Spartianus who says in his *Life of Caracalla*, cap. vii., that ' although the Egyptians call the moon a goddess, they really consider it in a mystical sense a god, both male and female.'[6] In the archaic Kemic belief as in the Euphratean, the Moon, Aah,[7] called Khons (' the

---

[1] *Juventus Mundi*, 323.   [2] *Fragment* xi.
[3] Cf. *Rig-Veda*, I. xcii. 4: ' Ushas [Êôs], like a dancer, puts on her gay attire' (ap. Muir, *Sanskrit Texts*, v. 185).
[4] *Od.* xii. 3, 4.   [5] Plutarch, *Peri Isidos*, xliii.
[6] Ap. Wilkinson, *Ancient Egyptians*, iii. 166.
[7] Cf. Ai (*sup.* Sec. VI.)   Aah = Copt. Ooh or Ioh.

Chaser '[1]) and Tehuti [2] (' the Measurer '), was pre-eminently male.

As noticed, Aiêtês, according to general tradition, wedded Idyia (' the Knowing '), a daughter of Ôkeanos. So Hyginus calls Mêdeia ' Aetae et Idyae filia.' [3] This wise Idyia is the same personage as Daeira (' the Knowing '), daughter of Ôkeanos and mother of Eleusis [4] (' the Coming ' Sun-god).[5] The wisdom from Ocean is primarily the light of the heavenly bodies who issue thence by day or night, as the case may be. This light is the earliest revelation. As regards the Moon generally, we may quote what M. Pierret says of the Kemic Lunus-Luna ;—' Champollion signale dans son Panthéon un Lunus *bifrons.* " La lune, instrument de la naissance, dit Hermès Trismégiste, *transforme la matière inférieure.*" ' This point is to be remembered in connexion with the Kirkê-myth. ' Cet astre, en raison de ses phases, est en perpétuelle relation avec les idées de naissance et de renouvellement. C'est ainsi que Lucine se confondait souvent avec Diane. Aah préside au renouvellement, au rajeunissement, à la renaissance.' [6]

The Moon as the Night-light, linked with Idyia-Daeira, is itself knowing and so appears as Mêdeia (' the Wise ').[7]

The children of the dark cold Air (Phrixos) and

---

[1] On this incident, vide R. B. Jr., *U.* secs. iv. xii. ; and cf. the angry and unsuccessful chase of the Argonautai by Aiêtês.

[2] Thoth.　　　　　　　　　　[3] *Fabulae,* xxv.

[4] Pausanias, I. xxxviii. 7.　　　[5] Vide *sup.* Sec. II.

[6] *Le Panthéon Égyptien,* 15.　　[7] Vide *sup.* Sec. VI.

the Copper-moon (Chalkiopê) are White (Argos) and Black (Melas), inasmuch as 'rebus nox abstulit atra colorem ;' Thought (Phrontis = Idyia developed), and some personage (Kytisôros) who seems to be of Akkadian origin.

Cicero happens to name Inô[1] ('the Bright'), otherwise called Leukotheê ('the White-goddess'), in connexion with Kirkê; and Inô is the third Moon-queen of the *Odyssey* who assists the hero. Daughter of the solar Kadmos ('the Easterner') she is the mother of Melikertes ('the City-king'), Melqarth, the Tyrian Hêraklês. As the White-goddess she is Lebhânâ ('the Pale-shiner') to distinguish her from the burning golden Athamas-Tammuz-Dumuzi. As the Rising-moon 'she came up from the deep, with-beautiful-ankle,'[2] foretells the escape of Odysseus, and gives him—Milton says she has 'lovely hands'—her 'immortal *kredemnon*,' the flowing scarf-veil, 'the line of waving light across the waters coming from around her face, and by means of which he may find his way to land.'[3]

The mythic pedigree of Kirkê, then, stands thus :—

---

[1] Inô = Iuno, Juno, a name akin to Zeus (vide M. Müller, *Lectures on the Science of Language*, ii. 496). Thus Janus was called Junonius.

[2] Cf. *Job*, xxxi. 26 : 'The Moon walking in brightness.'

[3] R. B. Jr., *G. D. M.* i. 258: vide *Od.* v. 333-53. The child of Inô the 'Bright'-moon, is also called Palaimôn, *i.e.*, Baal-hamon ('the Burning-lord'), the fierce diurnal Sun-god.

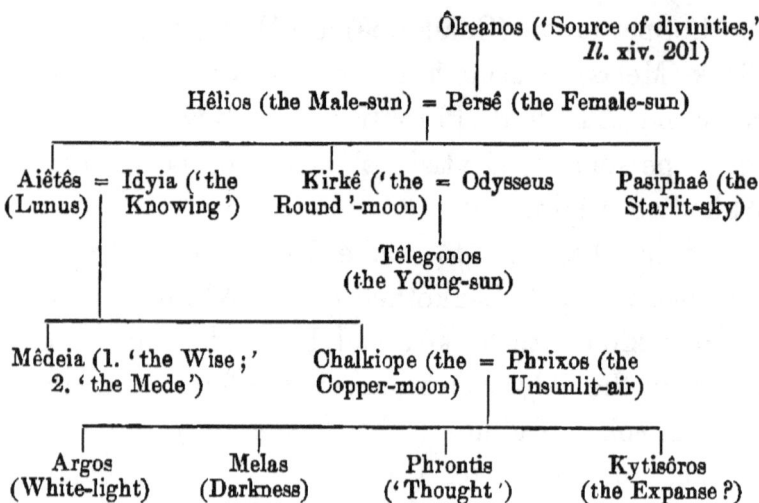

Ôkeanos ('Source of divinities,' *Il.* xiv. 201)

Hêlios (the Male-sun) = Persê (the Female-sun)

Aiêtês = Idyia ('the   Kirkê ('the = Odysseus   Pasiphaê (the
(Lunus) | Knowing')   Round '-moon) | Starlit-sky)

Têlegonos
(the Young-sun)

Mêdeia (1. 'the Wise;'   Chalkiope (the = Phrixos (the
2. 'the Mede')   Copper-moon) | Unsunlit-air)

Argos   Melas   Phrontis   Kytisôros
(White-light)   (Darkness)   ('Thought')   (the Expanse ?)

SECTION IX.

THE TRANSFORMATION.

THE party led by Eurylochos having drunk of the cup of Kirkê, are changed by her into swine ; and subsequently, pursuant to the prayer of Odysseus, ' became men again, younger than before and goodlier far.'[1] The idea is entirely unconnected with the theory of transmigration of souls, or with any idea of divine punishment inflicted on man for sin. The story of Queen Labe in the *Arabian Nights*, ' who, sensual like Kirkê, boasted an enchanted menagery of "horses, camels, mules, oxen," all retaining their human sympathies in their degradation,'[2] merits no special attention inasmuch as it is probably derived from the Homerik tale. The present story is also distinct from those which relate how the gods and other personages assumed animal forms in order to escape from their enemies,[3] or for purposes of deception. Thus a curious passage in one of the Izdubar series of legends, which records an archaic conquest of the city of Erech,[4] states :—

'The gods of Erech the Blessed
Turned to flies and concealed themselves.'[5]

[1] Vide *sup*. Sec. I. [2] Mayor, *The Narrative of Odysseus*, 138.
[3] Vide Ovid, *Metam*. v. [4] Vide *Genesis*, x. 10.
[5] Ap. Geo. Smith, *Assyrian Discoveries*, 169.

Kirkê acts in this particular manner simply because it is her nature so to do; and the basis of the myth is merely the effect of night upon the diurnal powers. Thus Prof. De Gubernatis well says, 'The hog is another disguise of the solar hero in the night—another of the forms very often assumed by the sun, as a mythical hero, in the darkness or clouds. . . . When the solar hero enters the domain of evening, the form he had disappears. He passes into another, an uglier, and a monstrous form. . . . The hero lamed, blinded, bound, drowned, or buried in a wood, can be understood when referred respectively to the sun which is thrown down the mountain-side, which is lost in the darkness, which is held fast by the fetters of the darkness, which plunges into the ocean of night, or which hides itself in the nocturnal forest.'[1] Such is the fate of the solar comrades of Odysseus. The sharp-tusked boar is, like the Sun, called Vishnu ('the Penetrator'); and the boar-shape is often taken by the Vedic Sun-god.[2] So the Norse Freyr ('the Lord'), the beneficent Sun-god, has his sacred boar Gullinburste ('Golden-bristle'). But 'this form is sometimes a dark and demoniacal guise assumed by the hero';[3] and so the boar becomes a monster of the night with lunar tusk and thus is hunted by Hêraklês and other heroes, or slays the solar Adonis.

'In Germany it is the custom, as it formerly was in England, to serve up at dinner on Christmas Day an ornamented boar's head, as a symbol of the

---

[1] *Zoological Mythology*, ii. 2.   [2] *Ibid.* 7 *et seq.*   [3] *Ibid.* 2.

gloomy monster of lunar winter killed at the winter
solstice, after which the days grow longer and
brighter. . . . The new sun is born in the sty of the
winter hog. . . . In the ancient popular belief of
Sweden, the wild boar kills the sun whilst he is
asleep in the cavern,'[1] the cave of Kalypsô. So the
subdued solar beings, the boars of day become the
hogs of night, are ' penned in the guise of swine, in
strong lairs.' But their intrinsic nature cannot be
destroyed and the return of day will restore them to
their former shape and beauty; and Kirkê herself
does this, for, as Arnobius has told us, she is the
mother of Hêlios-Sol.

' All around the palace wolves of the hills and
lions were roaring . . . bewitched with evil drugs.'
These creatures did not attack the comrades of Odysseus ; ' they ramped about them and fawned on them,
wagging their long tails.' The Wolf is especially the
creature of Night and Darkness;[2] the Lion of Day
and the Sun.[3] But both darkness and sun were
equally subdued by the bright lunar queen ; and
moreover, as noticed, it was just as likely that Kirkê
might have changed the explorers into wolves or
lions as into swine.[4]

The mythological connexion between Darkness
and monsters or monstrous animals is too familiar to
require any formal proof. The nocturnal dragons,
serpents, hydras, sea-monsters, demon-wolves like

---

[1] *Zoological Mythology*, ii. 13, 15.   [2] Vide R. B. Jr., *E.* 26.
[3] Vide R. B. Jr., *U.* Sec. xii.   [4] *Sup.* Sec. III.

Fenrir, or lions like that of Nemea,[1] form a long and formidable array; and in the Chaldaean account of the creation it is significantly stated that the primeval monster-animals were unable to endure the light and so perished. *Τὰ δὲ ζῶα οὐκ ἐνεγκόντα τὴν τοῦ φωτὸς δύναμιν φθαρῆναι.*[2] In the werewolf-myth, too, it is at nightfall that the possessed persons change to wolves, or that the wolfish instincts become overpowering; and the werewolf transformation approaches the Kirkê-legend, inasmuch as it 'is substantially that of a temporary metempsychosis or metamorphosis.'[3] But an Akkadian myth which is contained in the VIth Tablet of the Izdubar Cycle, if not exactly 'on all fours,' as the lawyers say, in its circumstances with the Kirkê-legend, yet is so thoroughly analogous to it and so perfectly explains it, that we see at once, especially when the Euphratean character of Kirkê is remembered, the basis and rationale of the Homerik tale. The solar hero Izdubar, an analogue of Odysseus, having come to great honour and renown, more especially by the slaughter of Khumbaba[4] ('the Maker-of-darkness') the Storm-cloud, the lunar and planetary goddess Tiskhu-Istar fell in love with him :—

'For the favour of Izdubar the Princess Istar lifted the eyes :
I will make thee Izdubar my lover,
Thou shalt be husband and I will be thy wife.
Into our house enter, mid the scent of the pines.'

---

[1] For an analysis of this myth, vide R. B. Jr., *E.* Appendix III.
[2] Berosos, *Chaldaika,* i. 6.   [3] Tylor, *Primitive Culture,* i. 279.
[4] The Κομβάβος of the tractate *Peri tês Syriês Theou,* which was usually ascribed to Lucian.

Similarly ' the palace of Khumbaba is surrounded by a forest of pine and cedar,'[1] and the dwelling of Kalypsô is ' a woodland isle,'[2] where, when Hermes arrives,—

> ' There came on him, as he stood,
> A smell of cedar and of citron wood,
> That threw a perfume all about the isle ;
> A sylvan nook it was, grown round with trees,
> Poplars, and elms,[3] and odorous cypresses.'[4]

And the palace of Kirkê is bowered in ' the thick coppice and the woodland,' and built amid ' the forest glades.'[5]

Izdubar makes a long reply to Istar and rejects her offer ; the first part of his speech is much mutilated, but something is said about a ' grand . . . tower of stone,' which agrees very well with ' the halls of Circe builded of polished stone.' He then proceeds to reproach the goddess with the illtreatment and evil fate which she had meted out to her previous lovers, who correspond with the metamorphosed companions of Odysseus :—

> ' As for Dumuzi the lover of (thy) youth,
> Year after year thou hast wearied him with thy love.'

The first lover of the frail Night-queen is the ardent

---

[1] Sayce, *C. A. G.* 221.   [2] *Od.* i. 51.   [3] ' Alder ' in original.
[4] Ap. Leigh Hunt.
[5] Mr. Keary, in support of his theory that Kirkê is a personification of Death (vide *sup.* Sec. V.), and having well noted that the name of her island (which like Taylor he connects with *alal*—' a land of such wailing as men utter by a grave') ' is also another name for Circê herself,' observes ;—' Circê's palace is buried deep in forest *gloom* ' (*Outlines of Primitive Belief*, 312). There is not a trace of ' gloom ' in the original ; the palace, though surrounded (not ' buried') with woodland, stood ' in a place with a clear prospect ' (*Od.* x. 211).

Sun, Dumuzi ('the Only-son'-of heaven), Tammuz-Athamas, who is wearied and wounded and dies.

> 'Alala, the Eagle, also thou lovest, and
> Thou didst strike him, and his wings thou didst break;
> He stood in the forest, he begged for wings.'

'The eagle we are told was the symbol of "the southern" or "meridian sun;"[1] the Moon-goddess however, Kirkê-like, strikes[2] him,' and the brave wings with which he flew so gallantly aloft are broken. He stands in the 'forest,' now familiar to us, and begs for wings that he might once more fly away on his solar path,=Odysseus intreating the moon-goddesses to let him go.

> 'Thou lovest also a Lion lusty in might,
> Thou didst tear out by sevens his claws.'

This 'bewitched' and subdued solar lion actually appears with his fellows around the palace of Kirkê. The Nocturnal-sun is sometimes represented as impotent or unmanned; thus the Vedic Indra 'disguises himself as a eunuch.'[3] 'To represent the evening sun asleep, a curious particular is offered us in the myth of Adonis. It is well known that doctors attribute to the lettuce a soporific virtue not dissimilar to that of the poppy. Now, it is interesting to read in Nikandros Kolophonios, quoted by Aldrovandi, that Adonis was struck by the wild boar after having eaten a lettuce. Ibykos, a Pythagorean poet,

---

[1] *C. A. G.* 246, note.   [2] 'Ράβδῳ πεπληγυῖα.
[3] Gubernatis, *Zoological Mythology*, ii. 2.

calls the lettuce by the name of eunuch, as it is that
which puts to sleep, which renders stupid and impotent ; Adonis who has eaten the lettuce is therefore
taken from Venus by the lunar wild boar, being
eunuch and incapable. The solar hero falls asleep in
the night, and becomes a eunuch, like the Hindoo
Arǵunas, when he is hidden ; and otherwise, the sun
becomes the moon.'[1] The heraldic Lion when in
this plight is termed *sans villenie,* and the line of idea
supplies a perfect explanation of the singular *caveat*
of Hermes to Odysseus respecting Kirkê, that she
must be sworn 'that she will plan nought else of
mischief to thine own hurt, lest she rob thee of thy
spirit and thy manhood, when she hath thee naked.'[2]
The hero subsequently reproaches the goddess with
entertaining this design ; she makes no attempt to
deny the charge and takes the oath as required.

' Thou lovest also a Horse glorious in war,
He yielded himself and thou didst weary his love overmuch.
For fourteen hours thou didst weary his love without ceasing.
To his mother thou didst send him wearied.'

In Aryan mythology the Horse frequently appears as
a solar animal, and again in Palestine we read of
' the horses that the kings of Judah had given to the
sun ' and of ' the chariots of the sun.'[3] The Horse
called in Assyrian *śuśu,* the Heb. *sûs,* is styled in
Akkadian *Imiru kurra* (' the Animal from the east ') ;
and this circumstance alone is calculated to give it
a solar connexion. Asva (' the Racer '), the Gk.

---

[1] *Zoological Mythology,* ii. 15–16. [2] *Od.* x. 300–1. [3] *2 Kings,* xxiii. 11.

ikkos (=*hippos*), the Lat. *ekvus* (=*equus*), has ever been naturally connected with the swiftly-moving Sun, the strong and jubilant race-runner. This further appears in the continuation of the legend:—

> ' Thou lovest also the shepherd Tabulu,
> Of whom continually thou didst ask for thy stibium.'

The Ak. *tab* means ' swift,' and *ul*, As. *kakkabu* is ' star ; ' it is a variant of the Ak. *mul*, ' star, brightness.'[1] *U* is the ordinary termination of the nominative in Assyrian; hence *ulu* or *mulu* = $\mu\hat{\omega}\lambda\upsilon$,[2] the mysterious Homerik countercharm to the charms of Kirkê,[3] and Tabul is ' the Swift-star,' the Racer-sun, original king and shepherd of the starry flock.[4] Istar thus next loves the Sun in his phase as the solar shepherd.

> ' Every day he propitiated thee with offerings.'

That is to say, just as an Oriental beauty heightens her charms with *stimmi* or *stibium*, a dark pigment with which the eyelids were stained and the eyes made to look more lustrous, so at the end of each day the sinking Sun brought with him that darkness necessary to set off in full splendour the beauty of the lunar eye, the brightness of the Moon.

> ' Thou didst strike him and to a hyena [5] thou didst change him.'

Here, again, the luckless lover is ' struck,' and this

---

[1] Vide Sayce, *Assyrian Grammar*, Syl. No. 169.

[2] *Od.* x. 305.   [3] Vide *inf.* Sec. X.

[4] As to the Ram-sun, the original Aries, and the starry flock, vide R. B. Jr., *L. K. O.* sec. x. So *Arcturus* is called in Euphratean regions ' the Shepherd of the heavenly flock.'   [5] Or ' leopard.'

time metamorphosed, exactly after the manner of
Kirkê, into a hyena or leopard; that is to say, into
some animal whose spotted skin symbolized the starry
vault of night. The Sun thus transformed becomes
Hêraklês Astrochitôn ('Starry-tunic'), Dionysos Nebridopeplos ('Clad-in-a-fawn-skin-robe'), but I have
elsewhere so fully illustrated the nocturnal character
of the spotted-animal that I will not now further
dwell upon this aspect of the myth.[1]

> 'His own village drove him away;
> His dogs tore his wounds.'

Fox Talbot, commenting on this passage, observes;—
'We see here beyond a doubt the ancient original of
the Greek fable of Actaeon and his dogs. That hero
had offended Diana [=Artemis-Selênê], who revenged
herself by changing him into a stag [=the spotted
leopard or hyena [2]], when his dogs, no longer knowing their master, fell upon him and tore him to pieces.
The great celebrity of this fable may be judged of
from the circumstance that Ovid has preserved the
names of all the dogs, though there were no fewer
than thirty-five of them.'[3] It cannot truly be said
that this view is 'beyond a doubt,' inasmuch as an
independent Aryan myth to the same effect might

---

[1] Vide R. B. Jr., *G. D. M.* ii. 19 *et seq.*; *U.* sec. xi.
[2] Vide Gubernatis, *Zoological Mythology*, ii. 83 *et seq.*
[3] *Records of the Past*, ix. 120; cf. Ovid. *Metam.* iii. 206 *et seq.*;
Hyginus, *Fabulae*, clxxxi.; Statius, *Thebaid.* ii. 203. Talbot's mythological speculations must be received with caution, just as in many cases
his translations of the Inscriptions are not up to the present standard of
Assyriology, but nevertheless he has done excellent service.

easily have arisen; but it is probably correct, more especially since Aktaiôn ('the Rayed'[1]), the son of the solar Aristaios[2] and of Autonoê ('the Instinct-with-sense'=Daeira and Idyia[3]), is the grandson of Kadmos ('the Easterner'=the Sun) and dwells in Boiôtia, so famous for its Semitic associations.[4] His paternal grandsire is Apollôn, and Prof. De Gubernatis thus comments upon the stag-myth ;—'The evening sun reflects its rays in the ocean of night, the sun-stag sees its horns reflected in the fountain or lake of night, and admires them. At this fountain sits a beautiful and bewitching siren, the moon; this fountain is the dwelling of the moon; she allures the hero-stag that admires itself in the fountain, and ruins it. . . The stag is torn to pieces by the dogs who over-take it in the forest because its horns become en-tangled in the branches; the solar rays are enveloped in the branches of the nocturnal forest. In Stesichoros, quoted by Pausanias, Artemis puts a stag's skin round Aktaiôn and incites the dogs to devour him ; '[5] that is to say, the spotted robe of night is thrown over the Sun and he is torn into small pieces (stars). This is one of the many aspects of solar suffering ; 'being torn or cut to pieces is a fate commonly ascribed to

---

[1] Similarly the hero Aktis ('Sun-beam'), son of Hêlios, was said by the inhabitants of Rhodos ('the Rosy') to have been the first astronomer (Diodoros, v. 57).

[2] Vide R. B. Jr., *G. D. M.* i. 402.

[3] Vide *sup.* Sec. VIII. According to the Neo-Platonists Autonoê represents the Air.

[4] Vide R. B. Jr., *G. D. M.* cap. x. sec. ii. Kadmos and Thebai.

[5] *Zoological Mythology,* ii. 86.

Dionysos and the personages connected with him, such as Zagreus, Pentheus, Orpheus, Uasar [Asar, Osiris], and others. Demosthenes is quoted as saying that the " spotted fawns were torn in pieces for a certain mystic reason," which, we are informed, " was in imitation of the sufferings of Dionysos." [1] Polygnôtos painted in the Leschê at Delphoi ' Aktaiôn, the son of Aristaios, and the mother of Aktaiôn, νεβρὸν ἐν ταῖς χερσὶν ἔχοντες ἐλάφου, καὶ ἐπὶ δέρματι ἐλάφου καθε-ζόμενοι· κύων τε θηρευτικὴ παράκειταί σφισι.' [2] The solar dogs of light turn at nightfall into dogs of darkness, werewolves, and devour their luckless lord.

The mythological Stag is on the whole a distinctly nocturnal creature, representing ' the luminous forms that appear in the cloudy or nocturnal forest,' which latter appears alike in Aryan and Euphratean myth. ' The mythic stag is nearly always either entirely luminous or else spotted; when it is black it is of a diabolical nature, and represents the whole sky of night.' [3] Thus it is when he is in the domain of the lunar queen that Odysseus slays that ' huge beast ' ' the tall antlered stag,' [4] upon whom ' the might of the sun was sore; ' [5] and in the incident obtains, as

---

[1] R. B. Jr., *G. D. M.* i. 152–3. [2] Pausanias, X. xxx. 2.

[3] Gubernatis, *Zoological Mythology*, ii. 83.

[4] This Stag was a very special and extraordinary one. Thus Odysseus fastens together the feet δεινοῖο πελώρου (*Od.* x. 168). This phrase is applied to the ' awful-looking Gorgô' (*Il.* xi. 36; vide *Ibid.* v. 741; *Od.* xi. 634). As I have elsewhere observed, ' It is not necessary to render πέλωρ "monster." The essential meaning of the word is " portent ; " cf. *Il.* ii. 321: πέλωρα θεῶν, "portents sent from the gods" ' (*U.* 47, note 1).

[5] *Od.* x. 157 *et seq.*

it were, a pledge that he should ultimately triumph over the nocturnal powers.[1] This view of the nocturnal nature of the stag is also in exact accord with the curious and repeated simile of Menelaos ;— ' Even as when a hind hath couched her newborn fawns unweaned in a strong lion's lair, and searcheth out the knolls and grassy glades, seeking pasture, and afterward the lion cometh back to his bed, and sendeth forth unsightly death upon that pair, even so shall Odysseus send forth unsightly death upon the wooers.'[2] The incident here referred to is not, so far as I am aware, in any way founded on any actual fact in natural history, and has every aspect of a proverbial saying. Like the heraldic beast-myths, such as the contest between Lion and Unicorn and between Lion and Leopard,[3] it is a phase of ' Zoological Mythology.' The nocturnal Deer couches her little spotted fawns in the lair occupied by day by the solar Lion, who returns in due course and slays them ; then, according to a Vedic poet, the abashed stars ' slink away, like thieves '[4] from the presence of Surya-Hêlios-Sol.

Another famous personage who was metamorphosed, and one, moreover, brought into relation with Kirkê who sends Odysseus to consult him, is the blind seer Teirêsias of the ancient family of

---

[1] The incident *may* of course be a mere arbitrary invention of the poet (It is servilely reproduced by Vergil, *Aeneid,* i. 180 *et seq.*) ; but I think that the more narrowly the poems are examined, the smaller will be the residuum attributed to this source.

[2] *Od.* iv. 335-40 ; xvii. 126-31.   [3] Vide R. B. Jr., *U.*

[4] *Rig-Veda,* I. 1. 2.

Oudaios ('the Chthonian'), son of Chariklô (= Charis) the daughter of Apollôn, Persês or Ôkeanos, a pedigree which has been already sufficiently illustrated. Teirêsias, who had been both male and female, who was blind and yet by the aid of his staff could practically see, and who has great place and power in the dark Underworld, appears to me to have been originally the Constellation-sky (τείρεα), blinded by Athênê the Dawn, but supplied with that golden staff, wand or sceptre so often found in the hands of nocturnal personages and which compensates for the eye of day. He is a Theban, for the knowledge of most of the constellations came to Hellas from Semitic sources; and Boiôtia was a principal point of intercommunication on the western mainland. And he is of a specially chthonian race, since the star-groups are closely connected with the Underworld.

The Istar-legend continues :—

'Thou lovest also Isullanu the husbandman of thy father.'

The father of the goddess is Ana ('the High'), As. Anu, 'the ruler and god of heaven,'[1] the analogue of the Aryan Varuna-Ouranos, and whose consort Anatu is the mother of Istar. I do not venture at present to attempt an explanation of the name Isullanu, but that like the other lovers of the goddess he was a solar personage is evident from the account. As to his being a 'husbandman,' Goldziher, who has traced

---

[1] *C. A. G.* 48.

with much learning and ability the intensely solar connexion of the myth of the origin of civilization, observes ;—' The founder of all the order and morality which result from the more civilized *agricultural* life is, in the language of the old stories, the Sun.' [1]

> 'Each day had he made bright thy dish.'

The sun by his daily retirement made bright the lunar disk, Istar being particularly, like Kirkê, ' the full moon.'

> ' The eyes thou didst take from him and didst put him in chains.'

The blinded Oriôn + the captive Odysseus. Isullanu complains, with the result that

> ' Thou didst strike him ; to a thing-hung-up [2] thou didst change him.'

Here is the usual blow from the goddess which in this instance, as in the last, at once produces a transformation.

> ' Thou didst place him also in the midst of the land . . .
> That he rise not up, that he go not ' [lines mutilated].

We are reminded of Odysseus fixed for long years in the island of Kalypsô, but it is needless to discuss the doubtful part of this remarkable account ; its general purport is indisputable and its connexion with the Kirkê-story very striking.

---

[1] *Mythology Among the Hebrews*, 201. The whole passage is well worthy of the most careful attention, and contrasts very favourably with the numerous crudities of the work.

[2] A ' pillar ' (Sayce).

The bewitched animals were used by Kirkê as house-guardians,[1] a circumstance which at once reminds us of the human-headed bulls placed at the gates of Assyrian palaces, and which as ' living genii ' were supposed to guard the gates of the Underworld in like manner.[2] So, on either side the door in the palace of Alkinoös, ' stood golden hounds and silver, which Hephaestus wrought by his cunning, to guard the palace of great-hearted Alcinous, being free from death and age all their days.' [3]

[1] Cf. *Od.* x. 434.
[2] Vide Lenormant, *Chaldean Magic*, 170.   [3] *Od.* vii. 91–4.

SECTION X.

SOME SPECIAL POINTS IN THE STORY.

HAVING considered the name, abode, mythic pedigree,
and special characteristic of the goddess, I will pass
on to notice certain minor yet highly interesting and
important details of the story, which, if the general
explanation previously given be correct, will all fall
harmoniously into subordinate relative positions.

I. *The habitual occupation of Kirkê.* 'They heard
Circe (1) singing in a sweet voice, as she (2) fared to
and fro before the great web imperishable, . . . fine
of woof and full of grace and splendour.'[1] Scholiasts,
both ancient and modern, who are prone to enter on
laborious investigations respecting the exact number
of the crew of Odysseus and a thousand other equally
weighty enquiries, are wont to pass such a statement
as this either without remark or with a feeble para-
phrase which repeats the original under pretence of
explaining it, reminding us of Young's complaint :—

> 'How commentators each dark passage shun,
> And hold their farthing rushlights to the sun.'

It is one of the chief difficulties of a modern investigator of the archaic to realize that there was a time

[1] *Od.* x. 221-3.

when many of the most ordinary incidents of our
human life, *e.g.*, speech, were regarded as wondrous
and semi-supernatural. The queen of witchcraft must
be also a queen of speech; her weapons are ' herbæ
et non innoxia verba.'; and this speech, like all archaic formal utterance connected with divinity, is
song, *i.e.* is distinguished by rhythm and assonance.
As the goddess is beautiful, so must her song be
' sweet '; there is no thought in the story of ' the
music of the spheres,' ' for ever singing as they shine.'
Speech, then, is wonderful, and is most closely associated with Religion,[1] and hence again with divinities.
We have only to recall such terms as *logos* (= Lat.
ratio + *oratio*) and *fatum* (' the spoken-word ') to
realize its awe-inspiring dignity. So in the *Rig-Veda*
' Vâc [= Vox, Voice], the sacred speech, is represented as an infinite power, as superior to the gods
and as generative of all that exists.'[2] I will further
illustrate the point by a highly suggestive quotation
from an able work by Signor Tito Vignoli :—

' Beginning with the traditions of our race, even
prior to its dispersion, there are plain proofs that
words and songs were originally employed for exor-
cisms and magic in various diseases, and for incanta-
tions directed against men or things. *Kar* means to
bewitch, as in German we have *einem etwas anthun*,
in low Latin *facturare*, in Italian *fattucchiere*, and

---

[1] Vide R. B. Jr., *L.* sec. i.
[2] Barth, *The Religions of India*; cf. *Rig-Veda*, x. 125. On this subject, vide R. B. Jr., *G. D. M.* ii. 325 *et seq.*

from *Kar* we have *carmen*, a song or magic formula. The goddess *Carmenta*, who was supposed to watch over childbirth, derived her name from *carmen*, the magic formula which was used to aid the delivery. The name was also used for a prophetess, as *Carmenta*, the mother of Evander. Servio tells us that the augurs were termed *carmentes*. The Sanscrit *maÿa*, meaning magic or illusion and, in the Veda, wisdom, is derived from *man*, to think or know; from *man* we have *mantra*, magic formula or incantation; in Zend, *manthra* is an incantation against disease, and hence we have the Erse *manadh*, incantation or juggling, and *mòniti* in Lithuanian. The linguistic researches of Pictet, Pott, Benfey, Kuhn, and others show that in primitive times singing, poetry, hymns, the celebration of rites, and the relation of tales, were identical ideas, expressed in identical forms, and even the name for a nightingale had the same derivation. So also the names of a singer, poet, a wise man, and a magician, came from the same root.'[1] The great enchantress is thus, like the great enchanter Homer, a mighty singer.[2]

Next, as to the great and 'imperishable web.' This, too, is a feature in the representation of Kalypsô. 'The nymph within was singing in a sweet voice as she fared to and from before the loom and wove with a shuttle of gold.'[3] Pherekydes of Syros, a writer

---

[1] *Myth and Science*, 306–7.

[2] As noticed (*sup.* Sec. II.), this is also a feature in the portraiture of Kalypsô.　　　　　[3] *Od.* v. 61–2.

of reputed Phoenician descent and whose works show
the strongest Oriental influence, supplies an excellent
commentary on the passage. He tells us ;—' Zas
[Zeus] makes a veil large and beautiful, and works
on it Earth and Ôgênos, and the abodes of Ôgênos.' [1]
Now Ogên, as we have seen, [2] = Ôkeanos, and this
brings the veil in very close connexion with Kalypsô
who dwelt in Ôgygia. The kosmic veil therefore represented Earth and Ocean, and the τὰ 'Ωγήνου δώματα = the δώματα Κίρκης, the dwellings of Kirkê,
Kalypsô, and similar personages ; for, as noticed, the
Ocean includes the Oversea. The web of Kirkê and
Kalypsô = the veil of Zeus, and is further represented in mythic legend by the starry peplos and
necklet of Harmonia, at whose marriage with the
solar Kadmos all the gods were present; [3] because
the harmonious union of Day and Night completes
kosmic order of which all divinities are the universal
champions and supporters. The veil, says Pherekydes, Zas hangs on a winged oak, even as Sir Tris-
tram tells Isolt that the ' carcanet' which he had won
at ' the last tournament ' was

' Grown on a magic oak-tree in mid-heaven.'

And Maury well observes on the myth, ' C'est là évi-
demment une image de la voûte du firmament, souvent
figurée par un voile, et auquel un arbre est donné
pour support. Il y a là une conception toute sem-

---

[1] Ap. Clemens Alex. *Stromata*, vi. 2.   [2] *Sup*. Sec. II.
[3] Apollodoros, III. iv. 2.

blable à celle de l'arbre Yggdrasil de la mythologie scandinave.'[1]   So, at Gabala in Syria was a shrine of the goddess Dôtô (Aramean Dôthô, 'Law,' *i.e.* Kosmic Order) who is also called Thurô (*i.e. thôrah*, 'the law '), and in the Phoenician Pantheon Khusarti, wife of the solar Khusôr ('Hûschôr) ; and, says Pausanias, ἔνθα πέπλος ἔτι ἐλείπετο.[2]   This goddess Dôtô-Khusar-this is identical with Harmonia,[3] ' the peplos-clad goddess of orderly arrangement.'[4]

Before the vast imperishable web of ' the eternal heavens,' the star-lighted splendour of space, 'fares to and fro ' the Moon-goddess ; and with this idea is necessarily connected the spinning of destiny, for Time in itself is but the transit of light in space,[5] and this light-transit brings on the fate of each.   So that when the Theban seer announces the hero's destiny Odysseus replies ;—

' Teiresias, all these threads, methinks, the gods themselves have spun.'[6]

II. *The Palace of Kirkê.*   As the abode of Ka-lypsô shows nature in her most charming aspect, so that of Kirkê shows the beauty and glory of art, and

---

[1] *Histoire des Religions de la Grèce Antique,* iii. 253.

[2] Pausanias, II. i. 7.

[3] On this subject vide Bunsen, *Egypt's Place,* vol. iv.; Lenormant, *Les Origines,* i. 519 *et seq.*

[4] R. B. Jr., *G. D. M.* ii. 238.   [5] Vide R. B. Jr., *L. K. O.* sec. ii.

[6] *Od.* xi. 139.   Cf. in this connexion the robes of Helenê, ' which she herself had wrought.' ' Helen stood by the coffers, wherein were her robes (πέπλοι) of curious needlework. . . . Then the fair lady lifted one and brought it out, the widest and most beautifully embroidered of all, *and it shone like a star* ' (*Ibid.* xv. 104–8).

is an artistic gem set in delightful natural surround-
ings. 'The fair halls' are 'builded of polished stone,'
the palace has 'shining doors,' and we read of silver
tables, bowls and basins, cups of gold and goodly
golden ewers, as characterizing the style of the equip-
ments of the 'great house.' Of course there is nothing unique in all this ; the palaces of Alkinoös and
Menelaos display the like, and the description is given
in stereotyped and conventional language. Thus in
all three palaces, as well as in that of Odysseus,
appears the 'grave dame,' who 'bare wheaten bread
and set it by them, and laid on the board dainties,
giving freely of such things as she had by her,' although certainly this good old lady, who 'found no
favour' in the hero's sight, was rather out of place in
the house of Kirkê, being very different from 'her
handmaids, four maidens' whom I shall notice subsequently, and being only referred to once and in
the above customary formula. Such descriptions of
dwellings and furniture are based, not upon the
imaginary foundation of poetic fancy, but upon two
utterly distinct sets of actual facts, each group of
which has been elaborately illustrated by a class of
writers ; and each of these two classes of investigators has been naturally prone either to ignore or
else to actually deny each other's standpoints and
discoveries. The terrestrial and historical basis of
the story is supplied by actual earthly wealth and
Oriental art in its westward progress ; whilst the
mythological basis is supplied by the splendour and

treasures of gold and silver and bronze possessed by dawn, sun, moon, and the light-powers generally. I do not think it needful to add a single word to the works of those writers who have so ably illustrated these two so widely different sources of Homerik description; but what I do venture to strongly insist upon is, that either source alone is quite inadequate to explain the fascinating mystery, utterly insufficient to support the wondrous superstructure.

The 'high seats' in Kirkê's hall, particularly the 'goodly carven chair' on which the hero sat, and which reappears on the Vases, perhaps demand a special word of notice in connexion with the lunar and Euphratean character of the goddess. The Akkadian Moon-god is styled Aku ('the Seated-father'), who, enthroned on high, is the special and chief supporter of nocturnal kosmic order.[1] The Moon-goddess 'fares to and fro,' 'walking in brightness;'[2] the Moon-god is seated in majesty.

Another noticeable feature in connexion with the abode of Kirkê, is that it lies in a marked manner beyond the sway of Aryan divinities. The only one of these who appears on the scene is Hermês, and his action here is in marked contrast with his proceedings in the case of the Aryan Kalypsô.[3] He is in direct antagonism with Kirkê and aids the Aryan hero against her, but secretly and as if half afraid to

---

[1] Kuu is the name of the Finnic moon-god, and Kua is a moon-name in Central Africa (vide R. B. Jr. *U.* 35).

[2] *Job*, xxxi. 26.   [3] Vide *sup*. Sec. II.

encounter her on her own ground. Still less has he any commands for her, and she sends away Odysseus and his comrades of her own free will. Kirkê is well acquainted with the Olympian divinities, but her position with respect to them is entirely different from that of their vassal Kalypsô; or, again, from that of Aiolos, who is 'dear to the deathless gods.'[1]

The palace of Kirkê, in accordance with Oriental fashion, had a flat roof, whence the young Elpênôr, whom Pope calls 'a vulgar soul,' fell and broke his neck.

The party remained enjoying the hospitality of the goddess 'for the full circle of a year,'[2] the grand lunar cycle.

The cup of Kirkê and its evil effects combined with her Euphratean character remind us of the striking words of the Hebrew prophet;— 'Babylon hath been a golden cup that made all the earth drunken: the nations have drunken of her wine; therefore the nations are mad.'[3]

III. *Kirkê's four handmaids.* As the Euphratean Sun-god has attending on him 'four divine dogs,' who represent the flow of solar radiance to the four quarters; so, similarly, the Moon-goddess is waited on by 'four maidens that are her serving women in the house.'[4] And as the Moon is the water-queen,[5] and mistress of the dark nocturnal forest in which she

---

[1] *Od.* x. 2. So Aiolos exclaims, 'Far be it from me to help or to further that man whom the blessed gods abhor' (*Ibid.* 73–4).

[2] *Ibid.* 467. [3] Jeremiah, li. 7. [4] *Od.* x. 349.

[5] Vide my analysis of the myth of Inô (*G. D. M.* i. 253 *et seq.*).

mostly dwells, so are these her handmaids 'born of the wells and of the woods and of the holy rivers.'[1]

IV. *The Mess or Potion.* This consisted of cheese, barley-meal, honey and Pramnian wine, + the un-named 'harmful drugs,' the whole forming the Κίρκης κυκεῶνα.[2] The compound, minus the drugs, was a well-known receipt, and so the 'fair-tressed Hekamêdê' prepared a like mess for old Nestôr and the wounded Machâon;[3] she 'grated cheese of goats' milk, with a grater of bronze' into the famous four-handled cup of ' Nestôr the Old,' in which the wine[4] had previously been poured. 'White barley' was then ' scattered' over this mixture, and apparently honey added according to taste. The mess constituted the Kykeôn ('That-which-is-stirred-up') or famous potion which Metaneira or Baubô gave to Dêmêtêr when wearied and exhausted with searching for Persephonê.[5] These potent drugs are more especially connected with non-Aryan regions. Thus Helenê obtains a store of ' medicines ' from ' Polydamna, a woman of Egypt, where Earth the grain-giver yields herbs in greatest plenty, many that are healing in the cup, and many baneful.'[6]

V. *'An awful goddess of mortal speech.'* This state-ment is a special item in the descriptions of Kalypsô

---

[1] *Od.* x. 350-1.   [2] Nonnos, xxii. 77.   [3] *Il.* xi. 624 *et seq.*

[4] According to Pliny (*Hist. Nat.* xiv. 54) the famous Pramnian wine was still made in his time near Smyrna.

[5] Vide the Hymn *Eis Dêmêtran*, 210; Clemens Alex. *Protrept.* ii. 20; R. B. Jr., *G. D. M.* cap. vi. sec. ii.   Dionysos at Eleusis.

[6] *Od.* iv. 228-30.

and Kirkê, and one which sorely exercised Aristotle,
as it has done numerous Homerik students since his
time. I do not think with the great philosopher that
the text requires any emendation; nor is it necessary
to repeat the various attempts at explanation which
the question of the speech of men and of gods has
provoked. An instance shall suffice;—' These inferior
goddesses,' says Mr. Mayor, ' living alone [?] in distant
isles, speak to men not by signs and omens, nor in the
language of the gods, but with common human
speech.'[1] This is merely a restatement of the case,
not an explanation; but, again, it is not an accurate
restatement, for (1) neither Kalypsô nor Kirkê lived
alone; (2) the inferiority of Kirkê (to what or to
whom ?) is much more easily asserted than demon-
strated; and (3) there is no Homerik ' language of
the gods' as opposed to that of men. This last fact
supplies the clew to the present difficulty. Because
the poet, in a few well-known passages, gives instances
in which some personage or thing (Briareus-Aigaiôn,[2]
Myrinê-Batieia,[3] Chalkis-Kymindis,[4] Xanthos-Skaman-
dros,[5] and the plant Moly) is known to the gods by
one name and to men by another, or is known to the
gods by a special name, it has been assumed that
the gods are supposed to have a special language,
whereas throughout the poems they invariably con-
verse with and are understood by mortals without any

---

[1] *The Narrative of Odysseus*, 139. [2] *Il.* i. 403. [3] *Ibid.* ii. 814-5.
[4] *Ibid.* xiv. 291. ' A kind of swift ' (R. W. Raper).
[5] *Ibid.* xx. 74.

difficulty, nor does the poet ever speak of any ' language ' of the gods.' The gods might well be supposed
to have special names (sometimes representing archaic,
sometimes foreign forms) for this or that, without
habitually employing a tongue ' not understanded of
the people; ' even if the action of the story did not
show irresistibly that such was the case. To revert
again to Mr. Mayor's remark above quoted. It further errs in that it assumes that the gods only ' speak
to men by signs and omens,' or in some ' unknown
tongue.' When Têlemachos whispered to Athênê who
was ' in the semblance of Mentês,' and ' the goddess
answered him : I will plainly tell thee all,' did she
speak in some strange and sacred dialect? Yes, it
may be replied, and he was by a miracle enabled to
comprehend it. But we must not add miracles to the
text; economy, not to say the law of parsimony, in
such matters must be studied. But it may be rejoined,
—This was a case of intercourse between a goddess
and a mortal; the gods amongst themselves speak in
their own dialect. Proof? Mr. Mayor further implies
that those divinities who lived ' alone ' had most occa-
sion to use human speech, which seems very strange ;
and also that the possession of the faculty of human
speech was a mark of inferiority. This last inference
the poet himself carefully guards against, for at the
very moment when Kalypsô and Kirkê are stated to
possess ' mortal speech,' they are styled ' awful ' as
if to negative Mr. Mayor's idea. What I understand
the poet to imply is simply this,—that even these

remote goddesses, far in the Outerworld, were an integral part of the general system of things, and had their special parts to play in connexion with mortals, and even with Hellenik and Achaian mortals ; that they, like their own Home-gods, could understand and be understood of men.

VI. *The plant Môly.* The previous topic naturally leads to the more special consideration of the ' herb of virtue'

> ' That Hermes once to wise Ulysses gave.'

' It was black at the root, but the flower was like to milk. The gods call it moly ($\mu\tilde{\omega}\lambda\upsilon$), but it is hard for mortal men to dig; howbeit with the gods all things are possible.'[1] This mysterious moly has been identified with the mandrake, chiefly, I presume, because 'it is hard for mortal men to dig;' and the mandrake's shriek ' when torn at night' was said to be fatal to the ears that heard it. Thus Southey makes the witch close her ears with wax, like the comrades of Odysseus when near the Seirens, and fasten a cord round the mandrake and round the neck of an ounce. The luckless animal

> ' Springs forceful from the scourge ;
> With that the dying plant all agony,
> Feeling its life-strings crack,
> Utter'd the unimaginable groan
> That none can hear and live.'[2]

But the mandrake, on account of its shape, has always

---

[1] *Od.* x. 304–6. Πάντα δυνατά ἐστι παρὰ τῷ Θεῷ (*S. Mark*, x. 27).
[2] *Thalaba*, ix. 22.

been regarded as a very special aphrodisiac,[1] a line of
idea entirely unsuitable to the case. We then turn to
Aryan philology; 'Curtius gives *mollis = molvis =*
Gr. μῶλυ-ς, akin to μαλακὸς. It would thus be related to the μαλάχη, *malva*, mallow, of Hes. *Opp.* 41.'[2]
But this explanation labours under the difficulty of
being inappropriate when the circumstances of the
case are considered; for the root-idea of *malakos,
môlos, môlus* etc. is softness, weakness, weariness and
the like, whereas the moly was a most potent talisman. Yet might not the ' soft ' plant have been such
a talisman ? Certainly it might, and the above view
may be perfectly correct; but if so, it is still unsatis-
factory since nothing is explained. Hermês gives
Odysseus the ' soft '-plant, by means of which he
baffles the enchantress. What is meant? It may be
suggested that the incident is merely a poetic fiction,
but he who would avoid the difficulty thus, reads his
Homer with but dim eyes. Again, the moly was a
rare and wondrous plant; the mallow is very common,
so much so that it was a usual article of food with
the poor. On this last point the mallow seems insufficient, for though it was constantly eaten, singularly
enough there is not the slightest suggestion that
Odysseus ate the moly, and this is the more remarkable since the baneful drugs were swallowed.
Now of course there are no baneful drugs at the basis
of the myth, since this is simply the effect of night

---

[1] Cf. *Genesis*, xxx. 14 *et seq.*
[2] Hayman, *The Odyssey of Homer*, ii. 158.

upon the world of day; but the moly or preservative of
the solar hero is a point in the basis of the myth, and
hence we see at once that what the moly represents
is not a plant but is merely symbolized by a plant.

I am well aware that my view of this incident
may be quite incorrect, and if Kirkê were an Aryan
goddess or even within the Aryan sphere, I should
not venture to propound it; but if there be any truth
in my standpoint, Kirkê is not only a non-Aryan but
actually a Euphratean divinity (and on this question
I must ask the reader to carefully judge the evidence
as a whole and not piecemeal), and therefore conjectures are allowable and even probable which otherwise would be out of the question. Sokratês, in the
Kratylos, when noticing Homer's remark ' about the
bird which

"The Gods call Chalcis, and men Cymindis." '

is made to say : 'There are many other observations
of the same kind in Homer and other poets. Now, I
think that this is beyond the understanding of you
and me.'[1] Yet the problem must be attempted, as
indeed it often has been; and it may well be agreed
that these double names show instances of archaic, or,
at all events, of old-fashioned, forms. But in the particular case before us there is no double name ;
μῶλυ δέ μιν καλέουσι θεοί. We may therefore fairly
examine the hypothesis of a foreign origin of the term.
And here be it remembered that, owing to contact

[1] Jowett, *The Dialogues of Plato*, ii. 213.

and importation, in all Indo-European languages there is necessarily a residuum of foreign words and names. Some of these are obviously foreign, *e.g.* βάλσαμον (*besem*), ἔβενος (*habni*), κίνναμον (*qinnamôn*), σάπφειρος (*sapir*), κάμηλος (*gamal*), μνᾶ (*maneh*), κινύρα (*kinnôr*); just as, conversely, we have *e.g.* Heb. *kvph* (Sk.*kapi*,ape), *habbim* (Sk.*ibha*, elephant). But others, though by no means obviously foreign, are yet really so. The following instances of the latter class occur, amongst others, in the Homerik poems :—

Aia (vide *sup.* Sec. VI.).

Aiêtês. (Ibid.)

Aigyptos. Ha-Ka-Ptah (' House-of-the-worship-of-Ptah,'—Brugsch).

Aphroditê. Aphrotet=Aphtoret=Ashtoret=Ishtar or Istar, the Akkadian Tiskhu (Fritz Hommel).

Assarakos. (Il. xx. 232 ; Vide R. B. Jr., *Eridanus*, 47).

Chalkos. Sem. *châlâk*, ʼsmooth.' ' De la racine *hhalaq*, " lisser, polir " ' (Lenormant).

Chitôn. Sem. *chthôneth.*

Chrusos. Sem. *kharouts*, Assyrian *khuratsu.*

Dardanos. The Ak. *dar*, As. *gisru*=' strong ' ; and the Ak. *dan*, As. *dannu*, also=' strong.' The Dardan (the Assyrian Tartan, Isaiah, xx. 1) is ' the Strong-one-of-the-strong.' [1]

Dionysos. The Assyrian Dian-nisi (' Judge-of-men ').[2]

---

[1] Vide further, R. B. Jr., *E.* 47.

[2] Vide R. B. Jr., *G. D. M.* ii. 209. I am of course aware that differ-

Erebos. A very interesting word and one familiar to Kirkê,[1] and as is now generally admitted,[2] derived from the Assyrian *eribu*, 'to descend' (as the sun). Its primary signification is the western gloom after sunset. *Europê* is *Ereb* the 'Western' side of the world, as the *Arab* is the dweller west of the Euphrates Valley. Thus the Cave of Skyllê is said to front ' towards the west, to Erebos ; '[3] Odysseus turns towards Erebos to sacrifice, and thence the ghosts assemble.[4] Heb. *erebh*, 'evening.'

Ilos. ' Son of Dardanos '[5] (vide R. B. Jr., *Eridanus*, 47).

Kadmos (*Od.* v. 333). Sire of the Kadmeioi and Kadmeiones of the *Ilias*. The hero from Kedem ('the East').[6]

Kêteioi (*Od.* xi. 521). The Hittites,[7] called by the Assyrians Khatti and by the Kemites Kheta.

ence of opinion obtains respecting many of these names, but must refer the reader to my previous writings on the subject (vide Reply to Prof. Max Müller on ' the Etymology of Dionysos,' *Academy*, Aug. 19, 1882).

[1] *Od.* x. 528.

[2] Cf. Sir G. W. Cox, *Mythology of the Aryan Nations*, 2nd edit. 151, note 2.

[3] *Od.* xii. 81.

[4] *Ibid.* xi. 37. The cuneiform ideograph for *eribu* is ⟨ ⊱⊱, which the Rev. Wm. Houghton (*Picture Origin of the Character of the Assyrian Syllabary*, 22) understands as ' a picture of the vault of heaven darkly shaded.' As the character ⟨ = (inter. al.) ' below,' and also for other reasons, I am of opinion that the ideograph is intended to show rays of light being swallowed up in the west (vide R. B. Jr., *An Examination of the Ideograph* ⟨⊱⊱, in *Proceedings* of the Society of Biblical Archaeology, May 4, 1880).

[5] *Il.* xi. 166.   [6] Vide *sup*. Sec. VIII.

[7] Vide Gladstone, *Homeric Synchronism*, 166 *et seq.* ; Sayce in *T.* vii. 254.

Kimmerioi. The Gimirraai.[1]

Kiôn.[2] The name of the Semitic Pillar-god, Dionysos-Stylos, Zeus Meilichios (=Melqarth, Melekh), Kronos-Kon, Heb. Kiyyûn (Chiun, Amos, v. 26), Arabic Keyvân, Assyrian Kaivanu, Hittite. Ken.

Krokos. Sem. *karkôm.*

Kronos[3] (= Karnos,[4] Karneios, Karnaim, ' the Horned '). As. KaRNu, Heb. KeReN. So Apollôn weds the Libyan nymph KuRêNê (' Horn ').

Kyparissos. Sem. *kopher.* So *kypros.*

Leôn. Sem. *layish.*

Oriôn. Otherwise Oarion and Urion. From Ak. *ur* ('light' and 'heat'), As. *uru* ('light' and 'day'), Heb. *aor.* Aorion-Oarion-Urion-Oriôn; also known in Boiôtia as Kandaôn (=Kohen-dian, ' the Prince-the-judge.' Cf. Dionysos).[5]

Persê (*sup.* Sec. VIII.).

Phykos. Sem. *pouk.*[6] ' Tangle ' (*Il.* ix. 7).

Poseidôn, Poseidaôn. According to Prof. Lauth Poseidôn is a Libyan god Badide. Certainly the name is not Aryan, but I think Phoenician, Tzur-dayan (' Judge-of-Tyre '), Lord-of-Syria.

Rhadamanthos (=Rhotamenti, ' King-of-the-hid-

---

[1] Vide *sup.* Sec. VI.   [2] Vide R. B. Jr., *E.* 78.

[3] As to Kronos, vide R. B. Jr., *G. D. M.* ii. 125 *et seq.* ' There is no such being as Κρόνος in Sanskrit' (Müller, *Selected Essays*, i. 460).

[4] Cf. Pausanias, I. xiii. 3: Ἀπόλλωνα ὀνομάζουσι Κάρνειον, ὑπὲρ τῶν κρανειῶν μεταθέντες το ῥῶ κατὰ δή τι ἀρχαῖον.

[5] For full treatment of the Oriôn-myth, vide R. B. Jr., *G. D. M.* ii. 270 *et seq.*; vide also Sir G. W. Cox, *Mythology of the Aryan Nations*, 380.

[6] Lenormant, *Les Premières Civilisations*, ii. 429.

den-world'). One of the few undoubted instances of borrowing from Kemic sources.

Sarpedôn. Darius I. in the Median Text of the Behistun Inscription enumerates among ' the countries which called themselves mine,' ' the Sapardes and the Ionians.'[1] The former are the Lykians, and Sarpedôn is ' the Sapardian.'

Thêbê, Thêbai. As to the Kemic city, the Nia of Assurbanipal and the No of the prophet Nahum, ' the Egyptian name of Thebes was Ap or Apé, the " head " or " capital." This, with the feminine article, became Tape, and in the Memphitic dialect Thape.'[2] The names of the cities called Thêbê in Boiôtia and the Troad are also non-Aryan in origin.[3] The same remark applies as of course to numerous Asiatic place-names found in the poems.

Mr. E. R. Wharton in his excellent *Etyma Graeca,* 1882, computes the words used by Hellenik authors down to B.C. 300 at 41,000, some 36,000 of which are compounds or derivatives. Of the remaining 5,000 no less than 641 are ' loan-words,' and 520 more ' are of doubtful or unknown origin, many of them indeed possibly foreign.' In his list of loan-words Mr. Wharton gives 36 ' root-words ' from Asia Minor, 92 Semitic, 46 ' Hamitic ' (Egyptian, Cyrenaic and Libyan), and 185 ' of unknown nationality.' The result, stated broadly, is that some

---

[1] Ap. Oppert, in *Records of the Past,* vii. 88.
[2] Wilkinson, *The Ancient Egyptians,* 1878, i. 61.
[3] Vide R. B. Jr., *G. D. M.* ii. 238 *et seq.*

500 out of the 5,000 words above mentioned are non-Aryan. Thus, setting aside the compounds and derivatives, $\frac{1}{10}$th of the Hellenik dictionary B.C. 300 (and I think that this estimate is rather under than over the mark) proves on examination to be Semitic, Hamitic or Turanian.

To return to the particular word in question. Prof. Sayce has noted that Apuleius Barbarus, ' a botanical writer of whose life no particulars are known, and whose date is rather uncertain,' but cir. the fourth century after Christ, states in his treatise *De Medicaminibus Herbarum*, cap. lxxxix., that ' wild rue was called *moly* by the Kappadokians ';[1] and Mr. Wharton who, like so many others, ' owes many invaluable suggestions to Prof. Sayce,' has included it amongst his Semitic (?) loan-words. But to what family did the language of Kappadokia belong, or were more languages than one spoken there? ' It is unfortunate,' says Prof. Sayce, ' that we know next to nothing of the language of the Kappadokians or of the Moschi, who lived in the same locality, and seem to have spoken a language allied to that of the Kappadokians and the Hittites ; ' and, again, he speaks of ' the Hittites of Kappadokia.'[2] But the language of the Hittites was probably allied ' to proto-Armenian and perhaps Lykian, and above all it was not Semitic.'[3] The cuneiform mode of writing was used in Kappa-

---

[1] *T.* vii. 284.   [2] *Ibid.* 285.

[3] *Ibid.* 287. Amongst other Hittite kings the king of ' the Arimai ' is mentioned in the Assyrian Inscriptions (vide *Ibid.* 292); cf. *Il.* ii. 783: εἰν Ἀρίμοις, ὅθι φασὶ Τυφωέος ἔμμεναι εὐνάς.

dokia at an early period, and Mr. T. G. Pinches has given a transcription of a Tablet from that country, now in the British Museum, and which he says, 'is written in a rather rough and peculiar style, approaching very nearly to archaic Babylonian. . . . The writing [of a similar Tablet at Paris] was extremely difficult to read, and the language seemed to be neither Assyrian nor Akkadian.' Both Tablets 'are written in a character distinctly Babylonian.' Mr. Pinches, in a further communication on the Paris Tablet, observes ;—'The question of the original home of the Akkadians is also affected thereby. . . . As it seems that the country north of Assyria was also called Akkad ['Highland'], as well as the northern part of Babylonia, the neighbourhood of Cappadocia as the home of the Akkadian race may be regarded as a very possible explanation, and the fact of the cuneiform characters being in use there would therefore be no mystery.' Mr. G. Bertin, having examined 'copies of both the Cappadocian tablets,' is 'satisfied that the writing is a dialect allied to the Aryan tongues, and especially to Armenian ;' and Prof. Sayce, when giving a 'tentative rendering' of one of the Tablets, declines to express any view 'pending the publication of more Kappadokian texts.'[1] I have not the slightest intention to rush in where these eminent authorities fear to tread, and t iis quite sufficient for my purpose to notice (1) that the Kappadokian language is not Semitic ; (2) that it is highly dubious whether even

---

[1] Vide *Proceedings* of the Soc. Bib. Archæol. Nov.–Dec. 1881.

by the aid of a liberal construction it can fairly be called Aryan ; (3) that it is written in the Akkadian character, but differs from the Akkadian language ; and (4) that it is very likely a variant Turanian dialect. The Paris Tablet contains the Akkadian words for *sun-god, maneh, shekel, god, man* and *woman.* On the whole, therefore, it is fair to assume a close connexion between (some) Akkad and Kappadokia ; and this connection may be linguistic, as well as political and commercial.

Having thus, I trust, shown the link between *moly* and Kappadokia, and between the latter and Akkad, the reader will perceive the historical and linguistic justification of the view already expressed,[1] *i.e.,* that in *moly (mul, ul)* we have an Akkadian word for which no equivalent was known to the poet. It remains to view the incident in its mythological aspect. We have already noticed that the moly in the story symbolizes something which, according to the etymology, must be a ' star.' Now it is unnecessary to search ' the mythology of plants ' for numerous instances in which the heavenly bodies are connected in idea with various plants and flowers ; it may suffice to mention the most common of simple flowers, the daisy (= day's eye = sun). The moly preserves and guides Odysseus, and what *watches over* the solar hero at night when exposed to the hostile lunar power but the stars ? and especially their

[1] *Sup.* Sec. IX.

leader and protagonist [1]—the Set-Sothis of Kem, Seirios ('the Scorching'), Sirius, ὁ τοῦ κυνὸς ἀστήρ,[2]

ὅν τε κύν' Ὠρίωνος ἐπίκλησιν καλέουσιν.[3]

As I have elsewhere [4] treated at length of the Oriôn-myth and of the star-guide of the nocturnal sun, I will here merely briefly recapitulate the instances:—

The Euphratean Izdubar, weary and leprous, is guided over the water by Lig-Hea ('the Dog-of-Hea').

The blinded Oriôn is guided by the dwarf[5] Kedaliôn.

In *The Great Dionysiak Myth*, vol. ii. pl. iv., I have given from a scarce and interesting work by Canon Spano,[6] a Phoenician representation of this latter incident. A blinded male figure of comparatively gigantic stature, with large wings outspread from the shoulders and holding a serpent in both hands, in manner very similar to the customary

---

[1] Ἕνα δ' ἀστέρα πρὸ πάντων οἷον φύλακα καὶ προόπτην ἐγκατέστησε—τὸν Σείριον (*Peri Isidos*, xlvii.).

[2] Hesychios, in voc. *Seirios*.   [3] *Il.* xxii. 29.

[4] *G. D. M.* ii. 277 *et seq.*; *E.* secs. iv., v.

[5] The protection of a house, the *door*, has preserved its primitive name in most of the Aryan dialects, Sk. *dvar*, Gk. *thur-a*, Lat. *fores*, Old Germ. *tor*, Slav. *dver-i*, and hence Sk. *dvarika* ('door-keeper'), Ang.-Sax. *dwerg*, Eng. *dwarf*, a word which acquired its present sense 'when that office was assigned to those whose bodily defects disqualified them from hunting or war' (Rev. D. H. Haigh, *Yorkshire Dials* in *The Yorkshire Archaeological and Topographical Journal*, v. 165). The stars are closely connected with the doors of the Underworld which they pass and guard (cf. the Kemic *seb*, 'star,' 'gateway,' vide R. B. Jr., *L. K. O.* sec. v.).

[6] *Mnemosine Sarda, ossia Ricordi e Memorie di varii Monumenti Antichi con altre rarità dell' isola di Sardegna* (Cagliari, 1864).

representations of Ophiouchos-Serpentarius which are
of course based upon the description of the constellation in the *Phainomena* of Aratos, bears upon his
head a dwarf or child-figure who, with keen eyes and
outstretched hands, is guiding his mighty friend.
Such is Sirius to Sol, whom he conducts through the
gloom of night, and Lig-Hea and Izdubar, Kedaliôn
and Oriôn, and the Moly and Odysseus are variant
phases of the myth. In this last instance the name
('star') is, as usual, the key to the position. Hermês,
pre-eminently the wind-power upon the clouds,
disperses the gloom and displays the Molu-star, a
friend of light, and, as a time-marker, a pledge of the
returning day, and hence of ultimate safety and
present preservation. With Sirius as with Teirêsias,[1]
the night-power who conversely has been blinded by
the day, but who at night and in the Underworld
recovers his potency, and who represents the awful
wisdom and might of the starry Signs, called in Kem
'the indestructible constellations,' the Sun can take
friendly counsel and be safely guided; the distant suns
protect their mighty brother in his hours of weakness.

　　The remarkable vitality of certain archaic names
and words is doubtless owing in part to a regard for
the principle laid down in a quotation preserved
by Psellos :—

'Ονόματα βάρβαρα μήποτ' ἀλλάξῃς,
Εἰσὶ γὰρ ὀνόματα παρ' ἑκάστοις θεόσδοτα
Δύναμιν ἐν τελεταῖς ἄῤῥητον ἔχοντα.

---

[1] Vide *sup.* Sec. IX.

So we find Iamblichos writing;—'You ask, "Why, of significant names, we prefer such as are barbaric to our own?" Of this, also, there is a mystic reason. Because the gods have shown that the whole dialect of sacred nations, such as those of the Egyptians and Assyrians, is adapted to sacred concerns; on this account we ought to think it necessary that our conference with the gods should be in a language allied to them. Because, likewise, such a mode of speech is the first and most ancient. And especially because those who first learned the names of the gods, having mingled them with their own proper tongue, delivered them to us, that we might always preserve immoveable the sacred law of tradition, in a language peculiar and adapted to them . . . If names subsisted through compact, it would be of no consequence whether some were used instead of others. But if *they are suspended from the nature of things,*[1] those names which are more adapted to the thing, will also be more dear to the gods. From this it is evident that the language of sacred nations is very reasonably preferred to that of other men . . . The Hellenes are naturally studious of novelty, . . . neither possessing any stability themselves, nor preserving what they have received from others . . . But the Barbarians are stable in their manners, and firmly continue to employ the same words. Hence they are dear to the gods, and proffer words which are grateful to them; but which it is not lawful for

---

[1] Vide R. B. Jr., *L.* sec. xvi. Occult Imitation.

any man by any means to change.'[1] Eusebius quotes
an oracle of Apollôn which declared that 'Many
ways of the Blessed-ones the Phoinikians, Assyrians,
Lydians and Chaldaean race knew.'

VII. *'The curious knot.'* When the Phaiakian
queen Arêtê had presented the hero with goodly
gifts, she recommends him to 'quickly tie the knot'
of the chest in which the presents were placed, 'lest
any man spoil thy goods by the way, when thou
fallest on sweet sleep . . . Odysseus forthwith fixed
on the lid, and quickly tied the curious knot, which
the lady Circe on a time had taught him.'[2] The
incident is altogether Semitic, and the fact that this
special knot was taught the hero by the goddess is
one of the many indications of her non-Aryan
character. The Phoinikians, as the 'common carriers
of antiquity,' were famous for the skilful manner in
which their packages were secured, a fact specially
noted by the Hebrew prophet when he speaks of
their 'chests of rich apparel [such as the 'robe and
goodly doublet' given by Arêtê to Odysseus and
placed in the 'coffer'], bound with cords, and made
of cedar.'[3] Both Jewish and Babylonian exorcists
used 'magic knots.'[4] The famous knot of Gordios,
cut by Alexander, was preserved at Gordion on the
southern border of Bithynia, a region where Aryan
and non-Aryan influences intermingle.

VIII. *The Passing of Kirkê.* When Odysseus is

---

[1] *Peri Mysteriôn*, vii. 4, 5.   [2] *Od.* viii. 443-8.
[3] Ezekiel, xxvii. 24.   [4] Vide Fox Talbot, in *T.* ii. 54.

with Kalypsô we read :—'So soon as early Dawn
shone forth, anon Odysseus put on him a mantle and
doublet, and the nymph clad her in a great shining
robe, light of woof and gracious, and about her waist
she cast a fair golden girdle, and a veil withal upon
her head.'[1] This statement is repeated in the case
of Kirkê ;—'Anon came the golden throned Dawn.
Then she put on me a mantle and a doublet for
raiment, and the nymph clad herself,' etc.[2] Having
so done, she disappeared ;—'Circe meanwhile had
gone her ways . . . lightly passing us by : who may
behold a god against his will, whether going to or
fro?'[3] Now 'Homer, like the author of *The Song of
Roland*, like the singers of the *Kalevala*, uses constantly recurring epithets, and repeats, word for
word, certain emphatic passages. That custom is
essential in the ballad, it is an accident not the essence
of the epic,' which 'still bears some birth-marks,
some signs of the early popular chant out of which it
sprung.'[4] Akkadian and Vedic Hymns enable us to
form an idea of 'the early popular chant' of Hellas,
and to see that it must have treated chiefly of the
ordinary phenomena of nature. In the case before
us, as the Dawn appears, the Moon arrays the Sun in
garments suitable to meet his love, and covering herself with the shining robe of day and veiling her face
disappears. There is nothing fanciful in such an
explanation, simply because the whole circumstances

[1] *Od.* v. 228-32.   [2] *Ibid.* x. 541-5.   [3] *Ibid.* 571, 573-4.
[4] Butcher and Lang, *The Odyssey of Homer*, viii.

of the case necessitate it. If we turn to a Vedic singer who is hymning 'the golden throned Dawn,' we find him using language which, after making due allowance for race-difference, is wonderfully similar :—

'Ushas [Êôs, Aurora] puts on her gay attire ;
  Directing her eyes towards all creatures,
  The goddess shines before them far and wide.
  She chases far away her Sister [*i.e.* Night, but in Homer Kirkê].
  The Lady shines with the light of her Lover [the Sun]. [1]
  The Sister [Night] has made way for her elder sister [Ushas]
  And departs, after she has, as it were, looked upon her [as did
    Kirkê] ;
  The bright goddess has chased away the dark veil of night.' [2]

If the poet had been hymning a beautiful Moon-goddess instead of a beautiful Dawn-goddess, the parallel would of course have been still closer. It is the dawn-moment when

'A silence fell with the waking bird,
  And a hush with the setting moon.' [3]

The *kalyptrê* ('cover,' cf. Kalypsô) or veil of the goddess is another phase of the *krêdemnon* ('head-band') which the lunar Inô gives Odysseus to save him from the deep, *i.e.*, the line of light thrown from the orb across the water. Dawn clothes the Moon in a shining robe and makes her invisible, and her bright *krêdemnon* folded over her fair face becomes a *kalyptrê*.

Miss Harrison remarks ;—'We have seen how strangely, in the Homeric conception of Circe, good

---

[1] *Rig-Veda*, i. 92, ap. Muir.   [2] *Ibid.* 113.
[3] Tennyson, *Maud*, xxii. 3.

and evil are intermingled ; how at one time she seems
a power of the baser sort, a sinister demon . . . at
another moment she is in very truth the daughter of
Helios, a goddess of light and strength, of comfort
and new life.' [1] And the apparent inconsistency of
character in this, as in a hundred other instances, is
explained fully by the Natural Phenomena Theory,
and by that alone.

[1] *Myths of the Odyssey,* 93.

SECTION XI

KIRKÊ AND THE NEKYIA.

Subsection 1. *The Voyage to Erebos.*

ANY account of Kirkê which did not notice her connexion with the Nekyia would be incomplete ; she
sends Odysseus there, gives him full directions, and
receives him on his return ; and although so much
has been said upon the subject, yet the Homerik
poems, like the plays of Shakspere, form an inex-
haustible quarry of material and invite the efforts of
every succeeding age. The standpoint already taken
will, I think, greatly clear up many of the very serious
difficulties of the story. Let us first view the matter
in the clear light afforded by the Natural Phenomena
Theory. At the coming of Dawn (Êôs) [1] the Moon
(Kirkê) retires (κεφαλῇ δ' ἐπέθηκε καλύπτρην), and
sends the Sun (Odysseus) in his (solar) barque with
his crew [2] for his day's journey (τῆς δὲ πανημερίης
τέταθ' ἱστία ποντοπορούσης) to Night and Darkness
(Erebos). The ship arrives at ' the limits of deep-
flowing Ôkeanos,' [3] which it crosses,[4] and disappears

---

[1] *Od.* x. 541.

[2] Called in Kem ' Ra's sailors' (*Hymn to Ra-Harmachis* in *Records
of the Past,* viii. 133).

[3] *Od.* xi. 13.   [4] Cf. *Ibid.* x. 508.

in the gloom. This is the extremely simple basis of
the myth, and I will next notice several special points
in the narrative.

I. *The direction of the Voyage and the points of the
Compass.* If we seek to wholly reconstruct upon the
terraqueous surface of the globe the wanderings of
Odysseus, we must be prepared to endure the gibe of
Eratosthenês that 'the scenes will be found, when
you find the tailor who sewed the bag of the winds,
and not before.' And yet I think that it is perfectly
possible to explain the Homerik idea of the wanderings, and to unravel certain difficulties well known to
every student of the text. Thus in the account the
Underworld-entrance appears to be in the East, a
day's sail south of Aia; yet according to the theory
above mentioned it must be in the West; and is not
Erebos, as the name itself imports, in the West?[1]
Most certainly. So the Shades of the Suitors were
doomed to go Ἐρεβόσδε ὑπὸ ζόφον,[2] and *zophos* is
the West, as the 'dark' quarter; they went accordingly 'past the flowings of Ôkeanos and the rock
Leukas,[3] and past the Gates of the Sun.'[4] The
flowings of Ocean and the gates of the Sun are of
course both eastern and western; but 'the rock
Leukas' shows, I think, unmistakably that a western
direction is indicated. So, again, Odysseus says
(incorrectly) that Ithaké κεῖται πρὸς ζόφον—αἱ δε [*i.e.*

---

[1] Vide *sup.* p. 83.   [2] *Od.* xx. 356.   [3] 'The White Rock.'
[4] *Od.* xxiv. 11–12. The passage, whether genuine or not, is in perfect
harmony with the rest of the poem when rightly understood.

Doulichion, Samê and Zakynthos] τ' ἄνευθε πρὸς ἠῶ τ' ἠέλιόν τε.[1] Ithakê faces westwards, and the other islands eastwards. Now I do not doubt that the apparent confusion arose thus:—In reality (*i.e.*, in mythological and natural belief) Erebos lies in the West, as is clearly laid down in the poems; but *historically* a great part of the material of the poet's story came from the (non-Aryan) East. Aia had a real actual eastern connexion in legend—the far region of Kolchis, although truly it was ' a floating island ' like that of Aiolos.[2] In this point of view, therefore, it becomes the place

ὅθι τ' 'Ηοῦς ἠριγενείης
οἰκία καὶ χοροί εἰσι καὶ ἀντολαὶ 'Ηελίοιο.' [3]

Similarly, the Κιμμερίων ἀνδρῶν δῆμός τε πόλις τε [4] is historically and actually connected with the same north-eastern region. Kirkê was well acquainted with

'Αργὼ πᾶσι μέλουσα, παρ' Αἰήταο πλέουσα,[5]

and the voyage of Odysseus from Aia is merely 'a reduplication of the voyage of the Argô from Aiêtês; in another work I have shown the Euphratean connexion of the Argô,[6] and also the connexion between the famous river Eridanos (Ak. Aria-dan, ' Strongriver ') and the Ocean-stream (Ôkeanos). Now in the poet's mind there is a vague idea of a voyage from the north-east—the region of Aia, Kolchis, and

---

[1] *Od.* ix. 25–6.   [2] *Ibid.* x. 3.   [3] *Ibid.* xii. 3–4.
[4] *Ibid.* xi. 14 ; vide *sup.* p. 33.   [5] *Ibid.* xii. 70.
[6] Vide *E.* Sec. V. Argô.

Kimmeria, down some great river-stream to the south
and south-west; and the basis of this is the archaic
Akkadian notion of a voyage down the Euphrates to
the southern region of death.

Let us, in further explication of the matter, consider next the Euphratean view of the four quarters.
Whilst Kemic pyramids except ' the step pyramid of
Sakhara ' which is very Euphratean in character,
were correctly oriented, Euphratean pyramidal temples
were oriented thus :—

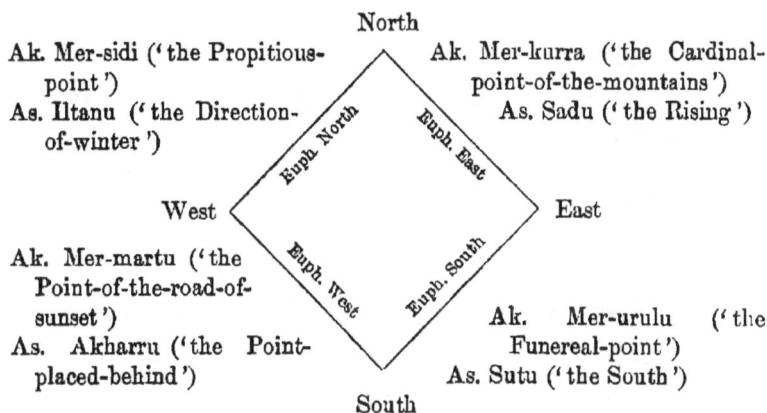

North

Ak. Mer-sidi ('the Propitious-point')
As. Iltanu ('the Direction-of-winter')
Euph. North
Ak. Mer-kurra ('the Cardinal-point-of-the-mountains')
As. Sadu ('the Rising')
Euph. East

West — East

Ak. Mer-martu ('the Point-of-the-road-of-sunset')
As. Akharru ('the Point-placed-behind')
Euph. West
Euph. South
Ak. Mer-urulu ('the Funereal-point')
As. Sutu ('the South')

South

Here the ' propitious ' North (N.W.) is opposite the
' funereal ' South (S.E.), *i.e.*, the direction of the
Euphrates to the Persian Gulf; hence a north wind
is the proper breeze for a voyage to the Underworld.
So says Kirkê :—

τὴν δέ κέ τοι πνοιὴ Βορέαο φέρῃσιν.[1]

The South and West are opposed to the North and
East, the two former being connected with Darkness

---

[1] *Od.* x. 507.

and all which that idea implies. So M. Lenormant says, 'The mountain of the west where the sun set, was a pre-eminently funereal place. A hymn[1] speaks of it in these terms: "The great mountain of Mulgelal,[2] the crest of which reaches unto the heavens, the sublime reservoir of water [Òkeanos] washes its base."' This is the mighty mountain Atlas in the far west.[3] 'The entrance to Hades was near this mountain of the west, or rather of the south-west,' and 'was also situated beyond the waters of the great reservoir of the ocean. . . The porter of the gloomy dwellings is spoken of as "porter of the waters;" and when he repeats to Allat[4] Istar's request for admittance,[5] he expresses himself thus :—

"These waters thy sister Istar has crossed them."' [6]

This mountain 'is invoked as a personal and active god (Ἄτλας ὀλοόφρων),[7] as the living mountain, in fact, which commands the entrance [of the Underworld] :—

"O thou who shadest the plain, lord who givest shade by spreading thy shadow on the plain.
Great mountain, who rulest destinies, who shadest the plain."' [8]

---

[1] *W. A. I.* IV. xxvii. 2.

[2] Mulge ('Lord-of-the-below,' *i.e.*, of the Underworld) is the analogue of the Semitic Bel and the Homerik Aïdês. *Lal* is merely a 'casual suffix.'   [3] Vide *sup.* Sec. II.

[4] The Ak. Ninkigal ('Lady-of-the-great-region,' *i.e.*, the Underworld), called also Ningiszida ('Lady-of-the-magic-wand.' Cf. the wand of Kirkê), the wife of Mulge and analogue of Persephonê.

[5] Vide *inf.* p. 112.   [6] *Chaldean Magic*, 168-9.   [7] Cf. *Od.* i. 52.

[8] *Chaldean Magic*, 171; cf. Macaulay: 'Where Atlas flings his shadow Far o'er the western foam' (*The Prophecy of Capys*, xxxi.).

Atlas rules destinies from his connexion both with the Underworld and with the starry vault which he upbears. Speaking of the Homerik Winds Mr. Gladstone observes that Boreas 'may be defined as a north-north-east wind,'[1] which thus appropriately blows the ship of Odysseus to the south-south-west and Underworld-entrance. The Homerik sunset, says Mr. Gladstone, verges 'though not perhaps with uniform precision, to the north of West.' To recapitulate, we have :—

1. The great solar voyage across heaven from East to West, an idea equally common to Aryan, Akkadian, Semite and Kemite, *e.g.* :—

(1.) *Aryan examples :—*

Hêlios in his solar boat-cup.

Hêraklês in the same.

Apollôn Delphinios.

Arthur in the barge.

(2.) *Akkadian example :—*

The voyage of Izdubar.[2]

(3.) *Semitic example :—*

The voyage of Melqarth in the West.[3]

(4.) *Kemitic example :—*

The voyage of Ra and the crew of his solar barque.

2. A confusion in the points of the compass, arising from the blending of Aryan and Non-Aryan

[1] *Juventus Mundi,* 477.

[2] For a consideration of this famous myth, vide R. B. Jr., *E.* sec. v.

[3] Vide R. B. Jr., *G. D. M.* ii. 286 *et seq.*

variant phases of the same great idea ; and from the incorporation into the story of certain circumstances more or less historical and actually derived from the Non-Aryan East.

II. *The Homerik Ôkeanos.* The following are the principal points in the Homerik presentation of Ôkeanos :—

As a personage he is called, in a recurring formula, θεῶν γένεσιν [1] ('source of deities') ; [2] and Sleep tells Hêrê 'another of the eternal gods might I lightly lull to slumber, yea, were it the streams of Okeanos himself, that is the father of them all.' [3] He alone of river-gods is absent from the great council called by Zeus ; [4] his consort is Têthys [5] ('the Nurturer'), an abstract personification. From him flow all rivers, 'every sea, and all springs and deep wells,' but he is not a match for Zeus. [6] The superiority of Zeus over him is thus twice distinctly and indeed with much emphasis asserted ; and the circumstance tends to show that he is a personage who might have been considered as a possible rival or in some way an opponent, in fact it is to some extent an indication of foreign connexion. Mr. Gladstone says that 'he alone is not called to the Great Olympian Assembly, because he could not appear there in his proper place, as head and Sire of all.' [7] He had also quarrelled with his Aryan spouse ; and Hêrê says, 'Their endless strife will I loose, for already this long time they

---

[1] *Il.* xiv. 201, 302.   [2] Gladstone.   [3] *Il.* xiv. 244–6.
[4] *Ibid.* xx. 7.   [5] *Ibid.* xiv. 201.   [6] *Ibid.* xxi. 195.
[7] *Juventus Mundi,* 345.

hold apart from each other, since wrath hath settled
in their hearts.'[1] The connexion between Ôkeanos,
Eridanos and the Akkadian Ocean-stream I have
considered elsewhere ;[2] and I think that in Ôkeanos
we have reminiscences of various Akkadian divinities,
most of whom were doubtless originally identical,
such as Ungal-a-abba ('the King-of-the-sea') and
Ungal-ariada ('the King-of-the-river'), but especially
of Hea, 'king of the ocean,' who arranges the reservoir[3] of waters around the earth, and who is 'god
of the house of water,' and 'lord of the deep.'

As the world-river, the ποταμοῖο μέγα σθένος
'Ωκεανοῖο is set by Hephaistos 'around the uttermost
rim of the cunningly-fashioned shield'[4] of Achilleus
which, I think, was round. The Dawn[5] and Sun,[6]
therefore, come from Ôkeanos, and on a special occa-
sion the former is stayed in Ôkeanos,[7] where also the Sun
sets.[8] The part of Ôkeanos whence he rose is called
the περικαλλέα λίμνην[9] (=*aestuarium*). *Sirius* bathes
in Ôkeanos,[10] but the *Bear* does not.[11] 'The Ethio-
pians that are sundered in twain, the uttermost of
men, abiding some where Hyperion sinks and some
where he rises,'[12] dwell by it;[13] and its southern
course seems to be referred to in the passage which

[1] *Il.* xiv. 206-7.　　　　[2] Vide *sup.* p. 98.
[3] *Apsu,* Ak. *zuab. Zuab-apsu* = ζὰψ ('the sea'), a term used by
several Hellenik poets quoted by Clement of Alexandria (*Stromata,*
v. 8).
[4] *Il.* xviii. 608.　　[5] *Ibid.* xix. 1; *Od.* xxii. 179; xxiii. 347.
[6] *Il.* vii. 422; *Od.* xix. 434.　　[7] *Od.* xxiii. 244.
[8] *Il.* viii. 475; xviii. 240.　　[9] *Od.* iii. 1.　　[10] *Il.* v. 6.
[11] *Ibid.* xviii. 489; *Od.* v. 275.　　[12] *Ibid.* i. 22-4.
[13] *Il.* i. 423; xxiii. 205.

declares that 'cranes flee from the coming of winter, and fly with clamour towards the streams of ocean,[1] bearing slaughter and fate to the Pigmy men.'[2] The ghosts of the Suitors go by the western portion of the Ocean-stream to Erebos.[3] The West being necessarily equally the home of light and darkness, there was a beautiful meadow by the western course of Ôkeanos where the Sun-god reigned amid happiness and splendour.[4] Ôkeanos 'floweth back ever upon himself,'[5] as the Jormungurdr and Weltumspannr; and his daughter Eurynomê[6] ('the Broad-spreading' light, =Persê[7]) receives and cherishes the infant Hephaistos (= Yavishtha, Juvenis), the young and weakly Fire-god, 'in the hollow cave[8] while around the stream of Ocean with murmuring foam flowed infinite.'[9] Pênelopê in her deep sorrow prays,

---

[1] 'Flowings of Ôkeanos.'   [2] *Il.* iii. 4–6.   [3] *Od.* xxiv. 11.

[4] *Il.* xvi. 151; *Od.* iv. 563–8.   [5] *Il.* xviii. 399.

[6] According to Hesiod, the mother of the Charites (Graces, *Theogonia*, 907–9); cf. Euryphassa, Eurydikê, etc.

[7] Vide *sup.* Sec. VIII.

[8] 'The misty eastern cave' (Shelley, *To Night*, i.).

[9] *Il.* xviii. 402–3. The 'broad-spreading' might in the abstract refer equally well to the spread of darkness, and so we encounter in the Leschê at Delphoi a painting by Polyguôtos of the chthonian fiend Eurynomos (=Tuchulcha, vide *inf.* p. 165) who was depicted dark blue with grinning teeth and sitting on a vulture's skin (Pausanias, X. xxviii. 4). Eurynomos was stated by the interpreters of sacred things at Delphoi to be a demon of Hades (locality), who was wont to eat the flesh of dead bodies so as to leave the bones bare. He therefore also represents the consuming power of the grave, and reminds us of the threat of Istar when about to descend to the Underworld, 'I will strike the threshold and will pass through the doors; I will raise up the dead to devour the living' (*C. A. G.* 239). Pausanias notes that Eurynomos is unnamed in the *Odysseia*, the *Minyas* and the *Nostoi*, although μνήμη δὴ ἐν ταύταις καὶ ᾅδου καὶ τῶν ἐκεῖ δειμάτων ἐστὶν.

'Would that the stormwind might snatch me up, and bear me hence down the dusky ways,[1] and cast me forth where the back-flowing Ôkeanus mingles with the sea.[2] It should be even as when the storm-winds bare away the daughters of Pandareus. . . The spirits of the storm snatched away these maidens, and gave them to be handmaids to the hateful Erinyes.' The western course of Ôkeanos seems to be here referred to, since, amongst other reasons, 'Erinys that walketh in darkness' dwelt habitually in Erebos;[3] and hence these maidens were snatched away to the Underworld by way of the western gloom.

It is probably impossible to recover the exact Homerik idea of the connexion between Ôkeanos and the Sea, and most likely for the reason that the poet had no exact idea on the subject. He is very precise when guided either by actual knowledge or by settled tradition and legend, but I apprehend that on this particular point he could have no support from either; hence studied vagueness. He knew of a great western sea; he believed in a world-girding ocean-stream. Hence if you sail far enough westwards on the sea, you necessarily come to the Ocean-stream, but in what particular manner is unknown; we naturally think of a connecting channel between the two, but none such is mentioned. The ship sails all day on the sea

---

[1] 'Ηερόεντα κέλευθα, the εὐρώεντα κέλευθα of *Od.* xxiv. 10.

[2] 'Εν προχοῇς δὲ βάλοι ἀψορρόου 'Ωκεανοῖο. All that is *said* is 'fluentis injiciat reflui Oceani;' and it may be doubted whether the passage *necessitates* any reference to the sea (θάλασσα).

[3] Vide *Il.* ix. 571–2.

and then simply came to the deep-flowing Ocean; again, it left the Ocean-stream and came to 'the wave of the wide sea.' There seems nothing to add to this.

III. *The mouth of Erebos.* Dismissed by the friendly Moon-goddess with the morning breeze (Aura-Aurora), the hero's vessel sails o'er the wide sea and into the Ocean-stream which it crosses;[1] and the crew having beached it, proceed on their way with the victims down the western or far side of Ôkeanos, 'till we came to the place which Circe had declared to us.' This place is thus described by the goddess;—'But when thou hast now sailed in thy ship across Ôkeanos, where is a waste shore of the groves of Persephone, even tall poplar trees[2] and willows that shed their fruit before the season, there beach thy ship by deep eddying Ôkeanos but go thyself to the dark house of Hades,[3] (thereby Pyriphlegethôn flows into Acheron, and likewise Côcytus, a branch of the water of the Styx), and thereby is a rock, and a meeting of the two roaring streams.' The sacred groves of the queen of the Underworld, who is herself both bright and dark,[4] are composed of poplars and willows; nor are these trees chosen arbitrarily or accidentally. The willow, from the Babylonish Captivity to the sad song

---

[1] *Od.* x. 508 with xi. 20.

[2] More correctly, ' tall black poplars' (αἴγειροι); cf. the 'black sheep' to be offered to Teirêsias, and the 'black ewe' presented by Kirkê for the sacrifice. 'Donabant nigro vellera nigra deo.'

[3] Aïdes, a person.

[4] For a consideration and analysis of the Persephonê-myth, vide R. B. Jr., *G. D. M.* i. 278 *et seq.*

of Desdemona, is connected with mourning, but this is not the idea in the archaic myth. The poplar is both black (as in this instance) and white, λεύκη, *populus alba*, sacred to the solar Hêraklês; and the willow ἰτέα, *salix Babylonica*, is similarly both black (μέλαινα) and white (λευκή). For the mythic groves of east and west [1] are both black and white (light, bright); the eastern grove black ere dawn,[2] the western grove black after sunset. The willow, moreover, is somewhat curiously linked with the direction of Kimmeria; for Herodotos says, ' The boats which come down the river to Babylon are circular. The frames, which are of willow, are cut in the country of the Armenians above Assyria.' [3] The premature shedding of fruit suggests the untimely descent of man to the Underworld.[4]

The Homerik text, as we have it, contains a curious specification of infernal rivers, jumbled up together in a manner at once utterly vague and yet unpoetical; and after careful consideration I feel bound to acquiesce in Dr. Hayman's conclusion, and at all events to reject the couplet

ἔνθα μὲν εἰς Ἀχέροντα Πυριφλεγέθων τε ῥέουσιν
Κωκυτός θ', ὅς δὴ Στυγὸς ὕδατός ἐστιν ἀπορρώξ.[5]

---

[1] For a consideration of the archaic myth of the Grove of the Underworld, vide R. B. Jr., *U.* 87 *et seq.*; *E.* sec. xxii.

[2] Ἀγλαὸν ἄλσος Ἀθήνης [= Ahana, the Dawn] αἰγείρων (*Od.* vi. 291-2).

[3] Herodotos, i. 194.   [4] Cf. Ψυχὰς "Ἄϊδι προΐαψεν (*Il.* i. 3).

[5] *Od.* x. 513-4. For full treatment of the question I must refer the reader to Dr. Hayman's laborious Appendix 'On the νεκυιά,' in his *Odyssey of Homer*, Vol. ii. Dr. Hayman notes from ' the Scholl. on κ.

By the dark groves there is a Rock ($\pi\acute{\epsilon}\tau\rho\eta$), which I would connect with the $\Lambda\epsilon\upsilon\kappa\acute{\alpha}\delta\alpha$ $\pi\acute{\epsilon}\tau\rho\eta\nu$[1] passed by the ghosts of the Suitors; for, though I by no means deny, but on the contrary assert, the connexion of the latter with the actual island Leukas, yet there is quite sufficient of the mythical in such a phrase as 'the White Rock' to extend its application beyond the limits of actual geography. The third mark of 'the place which Circe had declared,' is afforded by its being 'a meeting of the two roaring streams.' Now the well-known Homerik river of the Underworld is Styx ('the Hateful'), the fitting stream for the realm $\sigma\tau\upsilon\gamma\epsilon\rho o\hat{\upsilon}$ $\mathrm{'A\ddot{\imath}\delta\alpha o,}$[2] and, according to Hesiod,[3] the eldest daughter of Ôkeanos and Têthys; he calls her $\sigma\tau\upsilon\gamma\epsilon\rho\grave{\eta}$ $\theta\epsilon\grave{o}\varsigma$ $\mathrm{\mathring{a}\theta a\nu\acute{a}\tau o\iota\sigma\iota}$, recounts the story of the oath by the sacred water of the river,[4] and describes how one-tenth of Ôkeanos forms the Styx, which is $\mathrm{'\Omega\kappa\epsilon a}$-$\nu o\hat{\imath}o$ $\kappa\acute{\epsilon}\rho a\varsigma$ and $\acute{\rho}\acute{\epsilon}\epsilon\iota$ $\delta\iota\grave{a}$ $\nu\acute{\upsilon}\kappa\tau a$ $\mu\acute{\epsilon}\lambda a\iota\nu a\nu$ . . . $\grave{\epsilon}\kappa$ $\pi\acute{\epsilon}\tau\rho\eta\varsigma$[5] —the Rock already noticed; and the whole description, with whatever actual geographical circumstances it may have been partly connected, is in exact harmony with the Homerik account. Styx and Ôkeanos, then, are the two streams in question; and Kirkê calls them 'roaring streams,' a description for which I cannot find a parallel in the poems, the general view

513–4' that the names Kôkytos and Pyriphlegethôn 'were taken from the last offices performed upon the dead,' *i.e.*, the 'lamentation' and the 'cremation.' Neither of these names, nor Acheron (unless this be a variant of Acheloös), appear elsewhere in the poems.

[1] *Od.* xxiv. 11.   [2] *Il.* viii. 368.   [3] *Theogonia*, 361, 776–7.
[4] Cf. *Od.* v. 185–6.   [5] *Theogonia*, 788–9, 792.

of Ôkeanos being somewhat contrary to this idea. But in the Euphratean account of *The Descent of Istar* (Kirkê) *into Hades*, we find this exact expression applied to a river of the Underworld ;—

> ' To the roaring stream set thy ear ;
> May the lady [Istar] overmaster the roaring stream,
> The waters in the midst of it may she drink.' [1]

Now it is evident that there was some special peril connected with Styx, ' the dread river of the oath,' [2] for Athênê when angry with her sire exclaims ;— ' Had I but known all this, what time Eurystheus sent him [Hêraklês] forth to the house of Hades the Warder of the Gate, to bring from Erebos the hound of loathed Hades, then had he not escaped the sheer stream of the water of Styx.' [3] The actual Arkadian Styx is described by Tozer as ' a magnificent water-fall, which descends 500 feet over a stupendous cliff ; ' yet I do not think that the supposed downward course of the Styx of the Underworld was derived from this natural fact, but that the reverse process took place ; for the course of any Underworld-river which joined the Ocean-stream must of necessity be downwards from that point. In exact accordance with this obvious idea we read ' in the epic recital of the descent of Istar, that at the bottom of the country whence none return there was a spring of the waters of life, guarded by the infernal powers with jealous care ; which could only be reached by a special permission

---

[1] *C. A. G.* 244.   [2] *Il.* ii. 755.   [3] *Ibid.* viii. 366-9.

from the celestial gods, and then he who has drunk the water of the fountain returns alive to the light.'[1] Now amongst other Akkadian personages we meet with Khitimkurku ('The-spring-which-surrounds-the-sublime-mountain'), 'daughter of the ocean,'[2] like Styx, and very like her. The sublime Atlas-mountain which she surrounds has been already noticed,[3] and Hesiod says of the abode of the goddess ;—

$$\kappa\iota o\sigma\iota\nu\ \dot\alpha\rho\gamma\upsilon\rho\acute\epsilon o\iota\sigma\iota\ \pi\rho\grave os\ o\dot\upsilon\rho\alpha\nu\grave o\nu\ \dot\epsilon\sigma\tau\acute\eta\rho\iota\kappa\tau\alpha\iota,^4$$

just as it is said of Atlas ;—

$$\check\epsilon\chi\epsilon\iota\ \delta\acute\epsilon\ \tau\epsilon\ \kappa\acute\iota o\nu\alpha s\ \alpha\dot\upsilon\tau\grave os$$
$$M\alpha\kappa\rho\grave\alpha s,\ \alpha\dot\iota\ \gamma\alpha\hat\iota\acute\alpha\nu\ \tau\epsilon\ \kappa\alpha\grave\iota\ o\dot\upsilon\rho\alpha\nu\grave o\nu\ \dot\alpha\mu\phi\grave\iota s\ \check\epsilon\chi o\upsilon\sigma\iota\nu,^5$$

and as ' the Chaldaean Heaven rested upon columns,'[6] which must have been based in the Underworld.

Here at the $\nu\upsilon\kappa\tau\grave os\ \dot\epsilon\rho\epsilon\mu\nu\hat\eta s\ o\dot\iota\kappa\acute\iota\alpha\ \delta\epsilon\iota\nu\grave\alpha,^7$ ' the dread abodes of evening-night,' where $\dot\epsilon\pi\grave\iota\ \nu\grave\upsilon\xi\ \dot o\lambda o\grave\eta\ \tau\acute\epsilon\tau\alpha\tau\alpha\iota\ \delta\epsilon\iota\lambda o\hat\iota\sigma\iota\ \beta\rho o\tau o\hat\iota\sigma\iota\nu,^8$ we will pause a moment on the shadowy confines, and refer to an earlier descent.

Subsection 2. The Descent of Istar to the Underworld.

She who sent Odysseus to Erebos had been there herself; the Moon is familiar with the depths of the Underworld. There are two Euphratean accounts of the descent of Istar which have been translated by Fox Talbot, George Smith, and M. Lenormant. I quote from the revised translation by Geo. Smith :[9]—

---

[1] Lenormant, *Chaldean Magic,* 166.   [2] *Ibid.* 184.
[3] *Sup.* p. 100.   [4] *Theogonia,* 779.   [5] *Od.* i. 53–4.
[6] Gladstone, *Homeric Synchronism,* 231.   [7] *Theogonia,* 744.
[8] *Od.* xi. 19.   [9] 'K 162' (*C. A. G.* 239 *et seq.*).

' To the House of Assemblage [1] whence none return,[2] the land (of
    darkness),
Istar [3] daughter of Sin [4] her ear (inclined);
To the house of darkness the dwelling of the god Irkalla,[5]
To the house from whose entrance the light is taken,
The place where dust is their nourishment and their food mud.[6]
Light is never seen, in darkness they dwell.'

Smith renders the next line :—

' Its chiefs also are like birds covered with feathers ; '

But I prefer to read with Talbot :—

' Ghosts like birds flutter their wings.'

Talbot at first read 'bats' instead of 'ghosts,'
and we are strikingly reminded of the account of the
ghosts of the Suitors ;—' The souls followed gibbering. And even as bats flit gibbering in the secret
place of a wondrous cave when one has fallen down
out of the rock from the cluster, and they cling each

---

[1] Prof. Sayce reads 'Hades.' Talbot observes 'Hades is here called
Bit Edi, בית עדה, "the House of Assembly."' So *Job,* xxx. 23: 'I
know that thou wilt bring me to death, and to the House of Assemblage
for all living.' Talbot regards (and I think justly) the usual etymology
of Hades—'quasi A-ΐδης *invisible*'—as an 'afterthought.'

[2] Inasmuch as Aïdés is ἀμείλιχος ἠδ' ἀδάμαστος (*Il.* ix. 158), and
therefore will not yield them up again.

[3] 'Ishtar was the Full Moon [= Kirkê], for which reason she was
called the goddess *Fifteen,* because the month consisting of thirty days
the full moon was of course on the fifteenth day' (Talbot, in *T.* v. 102).

[4] The Moon-god. Moon springs from moon as sun to sun succeeds.

[5] *Ir* is 'to spoil;' *kal = dan,* As. *dannu,* 'strong,' hence 'judge '
etc. The meaning of *la* (⫻) seems to be unknown. Irkalla would
appear to signify 'Strong-spoiler,' the god of the Underworld as the
universal conqueror of men.

[6] Or 'clay.' *I.e.* where there is nothing to eat.

to each up aloft, even so the souls gibbered as they fared together.' [1]

'Over the door and bolts is scattered dust.'

The 'keeper of the gate' to whom Istar applies for admittance, is, as noticed,[2] 'keeper of the waters;' and there are 'seven gates of Hades,' a thoroughly Homerik expression.[3] There is also in the Euphratean Underworld 'the palace of Hades;' and equally 'within the dreary region [of the Homerik Nekyia] seems to be a palace, which is in a more special sense the residence of its rulers.'[4] Istar on passing through each successive gateway is despoiled of some ornament or part of her apparel, and regains them in a corresponding manner on her departure; for the Queen of the Underworld must needs release the Moon, who had gone below in quest of her husband-lover Dumuzi-Tammuz ('the Only-son'), the wounded and dying Sun, only son of the Sky. This whole account of the waning and waxing moon is replete with curious and interesting detail which will well repay the most careful examination.

Istar-Kirkê being the great love-power, her disappearance paralysed the life-course of the world:—

'With the cow the bull would not unite, and the ass the female ass would not approach, etc.'

---

[1] *Od.* xxiv. 5–9. So Shakspere: 'The sheeted dead did squeak and gibber.' So of the ghost of Patroklos: 'Like a vapour the spirit was gone beneath the earth with a faint shriek' (*Il.* xxiii. 100–1). The phantom form must have a correspondingly feeble voice.

[2] *Sup.* p. 100. [3] Cf. *Il.* ix. 312.

[4] Gladstone, *Juventus Mundi*, 373.

In a very similar account of the *Descent of Istar*
which is contained in the Izdubar Cycle, the goddess
says :—

> ' I spread like a bird my hands.
> I descend to the house of darkness.'

But there appear to have been in the Euphratean,
as in the Homerik, Underworld various regions of
widely-differing character,[1] for Istar continues :—

> ' In the house, O my friend, which I will enter,
> For me is treasured up a crown ;
> With those wearing crowns who from days of old
>   ruled the earth,
> To whom the gods have given names of rule.
> They drink limpid waters.
> In the house, O my friend, which I will enter,
> Dwell the lord and the unconquered one,
> Dwell the priest and the great man,
> There dwells Etana, there dwells the god Ner,
> (There dwells) the queen of the lower regions.'

In this connexion we are at once reminded of the
magnificent dirges of the Hebrew prophets over
great monarchs and others on their descent to
Scheôl. Thus Yesaya apostrophises the King of Babel
(Babylon = Bab-ili, Ak. Ka-dimirra, ' Gate-of-god ') :—

> ' Hell [Scheôl] beneath trembleth on account of thee—at meeting
>   thy coming,
> Arouseth on account of thee the Shades—all the leaders of the
>   earth,
> Stirreth up from their thrones— all kings of nations ;
> Thy bed beneath is rottenness, and thy coverlet is worms.'[2]

---

[1] Thus ' the mead of asphodel ' (*Od.* xi. 539; xxiv. 13), the special
haunt of the Achaian heroes, was apparently the choicest portion of the
shadowy domain.

[2] So in the legend of the descent of Istar we read :—' (There) dwell
the worms of the deep of the great gods.'

'To Sheôl wilt thou be hurled, into·the uttermost depth !
All the kings of nations every one—rest in honour each in his
house.'[1]

At the head of these throned phantom monarchs of
the dim archaic time sits ' the god Etana the king,'[2]
of whom Prof. Sayce observes ;—' He seems to be
the Titan of the Greek writers, who lived after the
Deluge and made war against Kronos[3] or Hea shortly
after the confusion of tongues. . . Etana ruled at
Surippak, the home and kingdom of the Chaldean
Noah.'[4] If the name Titan means ' King,'[5] then ' those
below Tartaros that are called Titans,'[6] ' the gods of
the nether world that are with Kronos,'[7] who were
once in the upper regions,[8] but were imprisoned by
Zeus beneath the earth,[9] and amongst whom Iapetos
is specially named,[10] are cast down ' kings ' (of something and somewhere) who reigned in upper realms
ere their fall.   But the expression οἱ Τιτῆνες καλέονται
may not improbably indicate a non-Hellenik name,
and the various Aryan conjectures from that
of Hesiod downwards are not very satisfactory.
Iapetos, again, is almost certainly connected with

---

[1] Ap. Ewald, *Commentary on the Prophets of the Old Testament*, iv.
241–2.

[2] Babylonian *Fable of the Eagle.*

[3]
　　Καὶ βασίλευσε Κρόνος, και Τιτᾶν, 'Ιαπετός τε,
　　Καὶ μαχέσαντο Κρόνος Τιτᾶν τε πρὸς αὐτούς
　　　　　　　(*Sibylline Oracles*, ap. Cory, *Fragments*, 52–3).

[4] *C. A. G.* 147.

[5] ' Prob. its root is the same as τίταξ = βασιλεύς, and τιτήνη = βασιλίς
in Hesych.' (Liddell and Scott, in voc.).

[6] *Il.* xiv. 279.　　　[7] *Ibid.* xv. 225.　　　[8] *Ibid.* v. 898.

[9] *Ibid.* xiv. 204.　　　[10] *Ibid.* viii. 479.

Yapheth (Japhet = As. Ippatu, ' the White-race ' [1]),
a name which carries us at once far beyond the
Hellenik cycle.[2] These beings were not seen by
Odysseus, for ' deep Tartaros is round about them ; ' [3]
and Tartaros is ' as far beneath Hades [where alone
he went] as heaven is high above the earth.' [4] Kronos
and his fellows are in ' the uttermost depth,' as
Yesaya calls it ; whilst elsewhere we read of sinning
angels that they were ' cast down to Tartaros, and
committed to pits of darkness.' [5] Ner (' Lord ' [6]) is
a second archaic and divinized king, and there is no
suggestion in the passage that their position was
penal, although it doubtless was sombre and solemn.
Euphratean Titans had been engaged in no contest
with an Aryan Zeus. It is a special assembly of
the great, and they ' drink limpid waters' from the
nether fountain.[7] We are reminded of the wish of
Odysseus who, after Hêraklês had ' departed again
into the house of Hades,' and although his legitimate
business was finished, yet lingered in the gloomy
region because his heart was minded ' to see the
spirits of those others that were departed.' [8] ' Yea
and I should have seen the men of old whom I longed
to look on.' [9] Who were these unnamed heroes of
the archaic time? But mere curiosity in such matters

---

[1] Vide Sayce, *Assyrian Lectures*, 145.
[2] Vide Lenormant, *Les Origines*, ii. pt. i. p. 173 *et seq.*
[3] *Il.* viii. 481. [4] *Ibid.* 16.
[5] 2 Peter, ii. 4. Revised Version.
[6] So Nergal = *Nir*, ' lord ' + *gula*, ' great.' [7] Vide *sup.* p. 109.
[8] *Od.* xi. 567. [9] *Ibid.* 628–30.

is ever left ungratified by the gods, and surrounded by myriads of the dead who kept surging up from the depths with inarticulate, wind-moaning, gibbering, bat-like clamour, the hero, no longer supported by duty although he had dauntlessly braved actual terrors, fled from a possible one.

As Yesaya has given us the grave-dirge of Babylon, Hezekiel supplies that of Kem with a corresponding gloom and sombreness which exactly harmonize with the Homerik and Euphratean Nekyia :—

> ' Strike up over the throng of Egypt the grave-dirge,
> And let her go down,
> Thou and the daughters of noble nations,
> Into the Underworld, to those laid in the grave !
> Into the lowest Underworld come thou !
> Let the first tyrants speak of him out of the belly of hell.[1]
> They went down, they lie slain of the sword.
> There is Assar and all her host, surrounded by her graves,
> All of them slain, who fell by the sword,
> Whose graves are set in the uttermost Scheôl,
> And whose host came round about her tomb.'

And there too is ' Aelam and all her throng,' and Meshek, Tubal, Edom, ' the crowned ones of the north all of them, and every Sidonian,' in fact ' the myriad tribes of the dead ; '[2] and around each kingdom, each leader, is his own special phantom host, even as we read :—' Thereafter came the soul of Agamemnôn, sorrowing ; and round him were gathered other spirits, all the men who had died with

---

[1] So Jonah prays ' out of the belly of Scheôl,' *i.e.,* ' the fish's belly.'
[2] *Od.* xi. 632.

him and met their doom.'[1] 'I died,' he exclaims,
' by a death most pitiful, and round me my company
likewise were slain without ceasing;'[2] in the words
of the prophet, 'They went down, they lie slain of
the sword.'

Subsection 3. *Aïdês and Persephoneia.*

The king and queen of the Underworld next
demand our notice. We may nearly always understand the Homerik term 'Aïdês' of a person rather
than of a place. A passage[3] speaks of Tartaros being
as far ' beneath Aïdês ' as heaven is above earth. But
when we remember that ' the Lord of the Underworld, Aïdôneus,' was usually seated on his throne
there,[4] it is evident that the passage in question is
equally satisfied if referred to a person and that it
does not necessarily imply a place. The ' halls ' of
Aïdês are ' grim, and vast, and lothly to the gods ;'[5]
and of the three Kronid brothers he ' is the third,
the ruler of the folk in the under-world.' He ' drew
the murky darkness ' by lot, when Zeus obtained ' the
wide heaven,' and Poseidôn ' the hoary sea ;'[6] and as
the majority of the Aryan divinities are the bright
beings who pre-eminently, and according to an oft-
repeated formula, ' possess the wide heaven,'[7] they
naturally abhor his dark domain. As I have said
elsewhere,[8] I regard him as being like Zeus, Hêrê,

---

[1] *Od.* xi. 387-9.   [2] *Ibid.* 412-3.   [3] *Il.* viii. 16.
[4] *Ibid.* xx. 62.   [5] *Ibid.* 65.   [6] *Ibid.* xv. 187-92.
[7] *Od.* xi. 133, etc.   [8] Vide *G. D. M.* ii. 251.

Dêmêtêr, Athênê, Apollôn, Artemis, Arês, and Hermês, an Aryan divinity. He is styled, in recurring formulas, 'mighty,'[1] 'having goodly steeds,'[2] and 'warden of the gate.'[3] His 'immortal horses' are mentioned in the Hymn *Eis Dêmêtran*,[4] in which he is called Polydegmôn ('the Much-receiving'), as all men descend to his realm; and Polyônymos, inasmuch as all nations revere a god of the Underworld, who has many names amongst many men. 'The Gates of Aïdês' are originally the two entrances (eastern and western) to the Underworld, and more particularly the western entrance.[5] The solar Hêraklês, who triumphantly penetrated to and emerged from the Underworld bringing up the dog[6] Kerberos (= the Vedic Sarvari, 'Darkness-of-night'), smote 'awful Aïdês' with a 'swift (solar) arrow in Pylos amid the dead;'[7] or, as Aristarchos well notes, 'at *the gate* of the Underworld;' that is to say, the conquering Sun overcame the gloomy power who guarded the portals of the Lower-region, and forced his way in. It was natural enough that such a legend should be localized at some place called Pylos, as Pausanias relates. He says that Athênê (the Dawn-power) aided Hêraklês, and that 'Hades' fought for the Pylians, because he was honoured by them and

---

[1] *Od.* x. 534; xi. 47.   [2] *Il.* v. 654, etc.
[3] *Ibid.* viii. 367; *Od.* xi. 277.   [4] V. 18.
[5] As I have elsewhere (vide *U.* sec. xi.) fully treated of the two entrances of the cave of Dionysos Dithyreitês ('He-of-the-two-entrances,' *i.e.*, the Sun), I shall not further notice the matter here.
[6] *Il.* viii. 368; *Od.* xi. 623.   [7] *Il.* v. 395-7.

'through his hatred of Hêraklês,' *i.e.*, the natural antipathy between light and darkness.[1] He is 'not to be softened neither overcome, and therefore is he hatefullest of all gods to mortals,'[2] in fact he is 'the Hateful-one,'[3] so detestable to man is death and darkness; and his name seems akin to that of the blind, sun-slaying Norse-god Hodr, Old High Germ. Hadu, Old Frank Chado, with which may be compared *odi, odium*, Sk. *vadh*, 'to strike,' from the root *wadh* 'to strike.' Hence, as Grimm says, 'the prevailing idea [in various forms of the name of Hodr] is plainly that of battle and strife.'[4] He is the smiter of life and light.

Mr. C. F. Keary remarks that the name Persephonê, 'which means light-destroyer, is as little appropriate to her whole character as Apollo, the destroyer, is appropriate to the sun god.'[5] Now there is almost invariably a supreme appropriateness in archaic names, and it is exceedingly unlikely that two very important divinities should be most unsuitably designated. I have elsewhere given reasons for understanding the name Persephonê as signifying 'Apparent-brilliance,' 'that is, the visible beauty-

---

[1] Pausanias, VI. xxv. 3. The fact that both divinities are Aryans, coupled with the exceedingly simple and appropriate explanation afforded by the Natural Phenomena Theory, negatives the idea that in this case a contest between the worshippers of rival cults lies at the basis of the story.

[2] *Il.* ix. 158–9.   [3] *Ibid.* viii. 368.

[4] Grimm, *Teutonic Mythology*, i. 223. Eng. Translation, by J. S. Stallybrass.

[5] *Outlines of Primitive Belief*, 242.

splendour of the material world;'[1] and as such, and in her character of Korê ('the Damsel'), she is snatched away by the dark king. In the same way there is no need to understand Apollôn as 'the Destroyer.' Welcker considers the Doric form Apellôn as the most ancient with the meaning of 'Averter;' whilst Prof. Sayce explains the name as signifying 'Son-of-the-revolving-one.' If Persephouê (as Hesiod calls her) had always been the queen of the Underworld, she might well have been named 'Light-destroyer;' but under all the circumstances of her myth this signification is absolutely inadmissible. The only fact connected with her which here requires notice is her remarkable prominence and potency in the lower regions when compared with the secondary part played by her great husband. And the explanation of this is at once perfectly simple, and also in absolute harmony with the general treatment of the myth here pursued. Mr. Gladstone, whose careful and searching study of the incidents and text of the poems is of the most material service to subsequent investigators, observes that long ago he 'had been struck by the predominance of a foreign character and associations in the Homeric Underworld of the Eleventh Odyssey. It lies, not in or near Greece, but in the region of the Outer Geography. The foreign goddess Kirkè, and the Kadmeian Seer Teiresias, are the sources from which Odysseus obtains his directions. The recent Hellenic

[1] *G. D. M.* i. 279.

Dead, furnished by the War, are wanderers in the Shades, without fixed doom or occupation, scarcely, as it were, naturalised in their new abode. None of the more ancient Hellenic or Achaian monarchs or warriors appear. And all, or nearly all, the characters, other than those from the Trojan Plain, are to be referred, either by the indirect indications of the Poems, or in consonance with general tradition, to a foreign origin.'[1] In fact the general concept is in the main borrowed, and Aïdês, who is known by many titles, represents a non-Aryan analogue ; whilst the name Persephoneia has been similarly applied to the Queen of the Underworld visited by Istar. This, too, has not escaped Mr. Gladstone who, when noticing the Istar-legend, says ; ' It is Ninkigal,[2] a Queen, who exercises the active functions of government in the Under-world; just as in Homer it is Persephoneia alone who acts, or is expected to act as sovereign below, while Aïdoneus is for the most part a mute figure in the background.'[3]

Subsection 4. *The Vision of Odysseus.*

And now Odysseus and his companions[4] stand on the perilous verge of the Underworld ; the trench is

---

[1] *Homeric Synchronism*, 213.

[2] Ninkigal = ' Lady-of-the-gloomy-pit' (Lenormant) ; or perhaps rather ' Lady-of-the-great-region,' *i.e.* Scheôl-Hades. She is also called Ninge ('Queen-of-the-underworld '), and in Assyrian Allat. Her husband is Mulge (' King-of-the-Underworld ').

[3] *Homeric Synchronism*, 235.

[4] Dr. Hayman's elaborate Appendix 'On the νεκυία' in the 2nd vol. of his *Odyssey of Homer*, is incorrect on this point. Odysseus is *not* said

duly dug, the drink-offering (mead, wine, water and
white meal) poured out, ' the strengthless heads of
the dead ' invoked, and the sheep sacrificed.[1]   When
cutting the throats of the ram and black ewe the
hero is to bend their heads ' towards Erebos,' and to
turn his face in the opposite direction towards
Ôkeanos,[2] *i.e.*, towards light and the east.   We must
next consider the questions (1) Did Odysseus descend,
or not? and (2) Did he quit his station by the
trench?[3]   On the first point Mr. Gladstone remarks;
—' Travelling over this rim [of land beyond Ôkeanos]
we enter the world of Shades, set beneath the feet of
the living, but yet accessible from, and without quit-
ting, the same surface as that on which we dwell.'[4]
So Dr. Hayman says;—' The whole is conceived by

in λ. 636 to ' rejoin' his comrades at the ship.   On the contrary he commands his ' company '—not merely Perimêdês and Eurylochos (vide *Od.*
xi. 23)—' to flay the sheep' (*Ibid.* 44), and subsequently Kirkê addresses
the whole ship's company as ' Men who have gone alive into the house
of Aïdês, to know death twice' (*Ibid.* xii. 21–2).

[1] With the interesting aspect of the story which is connected with
barbarous customs and archaic ritual, and associated ideas, *e.g.*, the
blood-quaffing by the ghosts, I am not here concerned.

[2] *Od.* x. 528–9.

[3] I assume, in order to avoid dwelling upon points and circumstances
often previously treated, that the reader is familiar to a considerable extent with Homerik literature on these questions, and on the Nekyia
generally.   Mr. Gladstone's *Homeric Synchronism* should be carefully
studied with respect to the Outerworld; and I would at the same time
add that I think nearly the whole of the explanations of Homerik names
in Prof. Lauth's *Homer und Aegypten* may be safely rejected.

[4] *Homeric Synchronism*, 230.   The reader will notice Mr. Gladstone's
remarks on the adoption by the poet of the Kaldean theory, that the
figure of the earth is 'boat-shaped' and hollow, the boat alluded to
being the round boat with sides curving inwards still in use on the
Euphrates (vide Diodoros, ii. 31; Lenormant, *Chaldean Magic*, 150).

the poet as enacted on a geographical extension of
the earth beyond the ocean stream. There is no
descent noticed, nor any passage of local description
denoting a subterranean position for the scene.' But,
he adds, ' Phrases are constantly in the mouth of the
poet which conflict with this his general conception.'
It would be strange if the poet constantly contra-
dicted himself as he went along, especially since the
general consistency of the poems is very remarkable,
and there are at least two passages which *do* notice a
certain 'descent' by the hero; thus he tells his
mother, ' Necessity was on me to come down εἰς
'Ἀΐδαο,'[1] and Achilleus asks him, ' How durst thou
come down Ἀϊδόσδε;'[2] but this ' coming down' is
not a descent into the Underworld as through the
crust of the earth, but a travelling downwards over
the ' rim' until he reached the edge of the Aïdès-
realm where he dug the trench. Mr. Gladstone's
account seems to me to be absolutely correct, as is
Dr. Hayman's except as noticed ; and we may take
it, therefore, as agreed upon that when standing by
the trench the hero had not lost sight of the night-
sky above, and had obtained a vision of a portion of
the Underworld beneath. The evening had closed
with a dark cloudy, ' deadly Night,'[3] the exact opposite of that starry and ' sign-potent Night' of whose
kindness to mortals Aratos dilates in the *Phainomena.*
Now Odysseus, although he had come to the realm
of Aïdès, never entered Erebos which, in the concep-

---

[1] *Od.* xi. 164. [2] *Ibid.* 475. [3] *Ibid.* 15–19.

tion of the poet (as distinguished from its etymological and archaic sense), is a deep and special part of the Underworld up from out of which (ὑπὲξ Ἐρέβευς) the ghosts ascended to the trench,[1] and into which the Hellenik hero-shades passed after their interview with Odysseus.[2] Next, did Odysseus quit his station by the trench? Dr. Hayman examines this question with much minuteness, and finding no sufficient cause for the final alarm of the hero except on the supposition that he had deserted his post and was a trespasser making a 'profane intrusion,' and therefore liable to chastisement by Persephoneia, suggests that Odysseus followed the shade of Aias in a vain attempt to obtain his forgiveness; 'but, he [Odysseus] in effect continues, "my attention was distracted from him by my curiosity about others;"' in fact he commenced to stare around like a rustic at a fair, the phantom hosts began to assume an 'altered bearing' towards him, and knowing he had no business there he precipitately retired. Dr. Hayman remarks that 'the whole account indeed somewhat labours under the double disadvantage of being at first somewhat diffusely spun out, and then somewhat abruptly cut short or "huddled up" at the close.' I do not think that the wonderful account labours under any such disadvantages, nor do I believe that in the poet's view Odysseus quitted his post by the trench, that his mind was easily distracted from one thing to another, that the ghosts

---

[1] *Od.* xi. 37. [2] *Ibid.* 564.

showed any 'altered bearing' towards him, or, lastly, that it is necessary to reject any part of the account as we have it. The crude objections of 'ancient critics'— *e.g.*, How could Minôs in his chair of state come forward and partake of the blood?—which Dr. Hayman refers to, and which he supposes would be satisfied by his theory, may be amusing as curious specimens of shortsightedness but are otherwise worthless. Thus it is neither said nor suggested that Minôs partook of the blood, and there is every reason to suppose that the poet would have stood aghast at the idea. But it would seem that Dr. Hayman regards Minôs, Tityos and Sisyphos as being supplied by the hero with the exhilarating beverage; and if we once begin to add to the account, it is easy to suppose that Odysseus (who was generally well provided with liquor) had filled a goat-skin at the trench and given them a drop all round, an attention which doubtless would have been much appreciated, especially by poor Tityos who, by the time that Polygnôtos had got him as far as the Leschê at Delphoi, appears, as Miss Harrison well remarks, to have been quite 'worn out,' and no wonder.

Let us examine the account on this point, for I lay much stress upon the position of Odysseus when he beheld the panoramic vision. We find him by the trench as 'the spirits of the dead' gather around 'with an ineffable cry' (θεσπεσίῃ ἰαχῇ), not loud, but strange, unearthly and savouring of the superhuman.[1] Though they are known to be 'strength-less,' yet warm flesh and blood naturally recoil; nor is the hero ashamed to confess 'pale fear gat hold on me,'[2] a remark which he repeats[3] with reference to the Gorgô-head, not to the supposed 'altered bearing' of the 'phantom hosts.' But he who never knew fear is equally destitute of the highest phase of courage, and this Odysseus had; and through the weird, gibbering clamour of 'these many ghosts,' clear and steady rings his commanding voice bidding his comrades 'flay the sheep.' Brisk occupation will serve to aid their trembling wits, for if pale fear touched that dauntless and daring heart, how felt the prudent, not to say timid, Eurylochos, and the common sailors? In front of the party, his drawn sword held steadily over the trench, 'sat' the hero, keeping the motley crowd of ghosts at bay. Before the grandeur of his presence his trembling followers, themselves doomed to a man to speedy death and darkness, are as nothing, and practically vanish from the scene. The ghost of Elpênôr approaches, and the two hold 'sad discourse, I on the one side, stretching forth my sword over the blood, while on the other side the ghost of my friend told all his tale.' The soul of his mother rises; Odysseus weeps, but yet with supreme and matchless steadfastness still guards the blood; tried to the utmost the

---

[1] So of the ghost of Patroklos we read, 'The spirit was gone beneath the earth with a faint shriek' (*Il.* xxiii. 100-1); 'a tiny feeble sound,' says Dr. Paley in loc., '*exilis vox*, as of a half-animate being.'

[2] *Od.* xi. 43.   [3] *Ibid.* 633.

refined gold bears the test, the sore moment passes,
and Teirêsias appears, bearing, like the Akkadian
Hades-queen Ningiszida ('Lady-of-the-magic-wand '),
'a golden sceptre.' The conversation with Teirêsias
ends, and the object of the dread journey is accomplished, for Odysseus only came 'down εἰς 'Αΐδαο to
seek to the spirit of Theban Teiresias;'[1] but, says
Odysseus, 'I abode there steadfastly,' and the conversation with Antikleia is then related. The hero
would probably rise to receive Teirêsias, and thrice
he sprang forward in a vain attempt to embrace the
shade of his mother; 'thrice she flitted from my
hands as a shadow or even as a dream,'[2] for, as the
Hebrew poet says, it is a rule 'since man was placed
upon earth' that 'he shall fly away as a dream, and
shall not be found;'[3] and as Antikleia herself says,
'The spirit like a dream flies forth.'[4] Next appear
the phantom train of 'the wives and daughters of
mighty men,' sent forth by their dread queen; for,
in exact accordance with Akkadian feeling,[5] great
prominence is given to females in the Underworld.[6]
Steadfast at his post Odysseus redraws his 'long
sword,' which he had sheathed at the coming of

---

[1] *Od.* xi. 165.   [2] *Ibid.* 206-7.   [3] *Job,* xx. 4, 8.   [4] *Od.* xi. 222.

[5] Prof. Sayce, apropos of a *Tablet of Ancient Accadian Laws,* observes
that amongst other things 'will be noticed the superior importance possessed by the mother. . . This importance of the mother in family-life
is still a distinguishing feature of the Finnic-Tatar race' (*Records of the
Past,* iii. 21). Cf. the high position of woman in Etruria.

[6] Mr. Gladstone's 'minute review' of this bevy of fair ghosts
(*Homeric Synchronism,* 216 *et seq.*) should be referred to. He remarks
that 'in almost every case we are able to detach them entirely from the
Hellenic stocks by Homeric or traditional evidence.'

Teirêsias; and suffers 'them not all at one time to drink of the blood. So they drew nigh one by one,'[1] and each tells her story. Persephoneia scatters them, and Agamemnôn and his company appear, followed after a while by Achilleus, ' a great prince among the dead,' and his three friends. Achilleus, ' rejoicing of his son's renown,' passes ' with great strides along the mead of asphodel.' 'The soul of Aias alone stood apart being still angry for the victory wherein I prevailed against him concerning the arms of Achilleus. . . To him I spake softly;' and, as Odysseus spoke, it would seem that Agamemnôn and the rest departed, but Aias ' answered me not a word and passed to Erebos after the other spirits of the dead. . . Even then, despite his anger, would he have spoken to me or I to him' yet further, ' but my heart within me was minded to see the spirits of those others that were departed,'[2] *i.e.*, not the personages whom he next did see, but ' some one of the hero folk who died in old time.'[3] With eyes grown far more accustomed to the darkness and fascinated with the wondrous revelations of the abyss, he says, 'I abode there still,'[4] *i.e.*, by the trench; there is not the slightest suggestion of any change of place. He did not venture to follow Aias to Erebos, but, as Miss Harrison well says, ' he seems to have sight into the innermost depths of hell;'[5]

---

[1] *Od.* xi. 232–3.   [2] *Ibid.* 566–7.   [3] *Ibid.* 629–30.   [4] *Ibid.* 628.
[5] *Myths of the Odyssey*, 115. Hell (' from the Teutonic base *hal*, to hide'—Prof. Skeat) = A-idês, and is therefore 'the Unseen,' 'the Hidden-place;' Aryan roots, *kal, kar, skar,* 'to cover.' Personified in

'the shades are there, guests in the depths of Scheôl.'[1] The ancient Hellenik heroes are unseen,[2] and, if v. 631 be spurious, are unnamed; but he had a vision grand and awful;—'I saw Minos . . . I marked Orion . . . I saw Tityos . . . I beheld Tantalos . . . I beheld Sisyphos . . . I descried Herakles.' But what had he to do with these wondrous monuments of grandeur or of woe? Was not his purpose accomplished, his mission fulfilled, and is it lawful for mortal without divine authority to tread the realm of Aïdôneus? 'Have the gates of death been revealed unto thee? or hast thou seen the doors of the shadow of death,'[3] when thou camest 'beneath the darkness and the shadow,'[4] but that thou mightest know the secrets of the 'prison house'? Nay, but that thou mightest know thine own destiny in the Upperworld; linger not here through curiosity, however wondrous may be the lore. It is unlawful, dangerous so to do; the awful queen of the shades may resent and punish—'straightway then I went to the ship.'[5]

The Book of *Job*, which has already been quoted in this connexion, presents a remarkable agreement with the Homerik theory and aspect of the Underworld. There, too, we meet with 'the pillars of heaven;'[6] with two divisions of the Underworld

the Norse goddess Hel, who again became 'only the home of the dead' (Keary, *Outlines of Primitive Belief*, 270).

[1] *Proverbs*, ix. 18.
[2] On this point, vide Gladstone, *Homeric Synchronism*, 213, 220.
[3] *Job*, xxxviii. 16, 17.   [4] *Od*. xi. 155.   [5] *Ibid*. 636.
[6] *Job*, xxvi. 11. Vide *sup*. p. 110.

Scheôl and Abaddon [1] ('the Place-of-destruction') which correspond with Hades-Erebos and Tartaros; with 'the bars of Scheôl;'[2] with the idea of being 'hidden' away in Scheôl;'[3] with the discovery of 'deep things out of darkness,' and the bringing 'out to light the shadow of death;'[4] and with the dreary region itself as 'a land of gloom, as obscurity itself, of the shadow of death, and of disorder, and where the light is as obscurity.'[5] Life is consumed as the cloud,[6] and as smoke, and vanishes like the shadow. And in *Job*, too, we meet with the constellation-band [7] (Mazzaroth-Teirêsias), by means of which the Sun is enabled to know his future destiny.

Subsection 5. *Some incidents in the Vision.*

Let us now leave the human interest of the poem with its splendid play of light and shade, and turn again to the task of further explication of the ideas; forget Odysseus and remember the Sun, whom we find on the margin of the dark world below, but not wholly out of sight of the nocturnal sky. Now two distinct, yet not inharmonious, elements enter into the entire presentation, and point to its basis as rooted

---

[1] *Job*, xxvi. 6. So we read elsewhere, 'Scheôl and Abaddon are never full' (*Proverbs*, xxviii. 20). Mulge (vide *sup*. p. 100) is also styled in an Akkadian Hymn Anunna-ge ('the Archangel-of-the-abyss,' vide Lenormant, *Chaldean Magic*, 164); and, similarly, we read of 'the Angel of the abyss, whose name in the Hebrew tongue is Abaddon, but in the Greek tongue hath his name Apollyon' ('Destroyer,' *Apoc*. ix. 11). Abaddon and Death have heard only a report of Wisdom (*Job*, xxviii. 22), for 'there is no wisdom in Scheôl' (*Ecclesiastes*, ix. 10).

[2] *Job*, xvii. 16.   [3] *Ibid*. xiv. 13.   [4] *Ibid*. xii. 22.
[5] *Ibid*. x. 21-2.   [6] *Ibid*. vii. 9.   [7] *Ibid*. xxxviii. 32.

in a remote antiquity; we have before us the Underworld *and* Night. The very word Erebos (evening-
gloom) stands between them as a connecting link.
Aryan and Akkadian had an equal, a remarkable
horror of darkness;[1] and here, as in the Vedic and
Akkadian Hymns, we see glimpses of a period when
the primeval chaos, the recurring night, and the
gloom and confusion of the infernal abyss, were
closely linked together in idea. It is evening when
Odysseus reaches the confines of the Underworld;
' the sun sank and all the ways were darkened.'[2] At
first ' deadly night is outspread ' above, but as the
night progresses it brightens; the starry Signs
headed by Teirêsias pass before the extinguished
Sun in the vast nocturnal cave. He sees Oriôn and
Hêraklês, solar phases reduplicated in constellations,[3]
and the latter appearing in a phase which reminds
us of *Sagittarius*; he notices various aspects of himself—Minôs, Tantalos, Sisyphos; no offence is laid to
the charge of the two latter, for they had in truth
done no wrong, their sufferings being but an anthropomorphic aspect of solar existence, and the moral,
now so hard to dissociate, being merely the afterthought of devout reflexion and natural religion.
And this fact, so simple yet perhaps somewhat new,
is made still clearer by the case of their comrade in
woe Tityos (' the Extended '), whose crime is named;
his offence was not moral or religious but mytho-

---

[1] Vide Lenormant, *Chaldean Magic*, 178.   [2] *Od.* xi. 12.
[3] Vide R. B. Jr., *E.* sec. x. Illustration of the Law of Reduplication.

logical. The stellar giant had laid profane hands on
that holy and kosmic darkness (Lêtô), the spouse of
the heavenly Zeus, the mother of Apollôn and Artemis, of Sun and Moon. The Twins, too, Kastôr
and Polydeukês, whose mother Lêda, a variant of
Lêtô, actually appears before Odysseus, though not
mentioned as being seen, are also referred to ; as is
likewise the Euphratean Sun-god Dionysos.[1]

If in Tyrô [2] ' we have the only indication, which
the Poems afford, of the afterwards famous historic
name of Tyre,'[3] we may well compare the name of
her sire Salmôneus with that of Zalmunna, a chief
of ' the hosts of the children of the east,'[4] a name
which perhaps reappears in Thelmanna the Kemic
form of a Hittite name. Nor is the connexion
weakened when we find that Salmôneus is the
brother of Athamas (*i.e.*, Tammuz-Dumuzi),[5] and the
husband of Sidêrô, ' step-mother of Tyro,' a personage who recalls Sidê, the wife of Oriôn, sent by
Hêrê to the Underworld because she presumed to
rival her in beauty.[6] Surely we are here reminded

---

[1] *Od.* xi. 325. Dionysos, *i.e.*, the Dian-nisi (' Judge-of-men '), like
Minós, is again named when a scene in the Underworld is represented
(*Od.* xxiv. 74).

[2] *Od.* xi. 235.   [3] Gladstone, *Homeric Synchronism*, 216.

[4] *Judges*, viii. 10.

[5] This identification which I first proposed in the *G. D. M.* i. 249,
has been accepted both by Prof. Sayce and by Sir G. W. Cox (vide R.
B. Jr., *U.* 28), as respective guardians of Euphratean and Aryan
interests.

[6] The student must carefully distinguish between the mythological
contests and disputes of divinities, and the ethnic and historical contests
and disputes of nations and religions, which are very frequently draped
in a mythological form. The character and origin of the particular per-

of 'great Zidon,'[1] and of 'the strong city Tyre,'[2] 'full of wisdom and perfect in beauty,'[3] yet brought down, as in the visions of Odysseus and Hezekiel, 'to Scheôl, to the recesses of the pit.'[4] But referring the reader to the careful pages of Mr. Gladstone's *Homeric Synchronism* for constant and remarkable illustration of the general foreign character of the personages mentioned in the Eleventh Odyssey, I pass on to notice more particularly several special incidents in the narration.

I. *The case of Elpênôr.* Patroklos the friend of Achilleus and Elpênôr the comrade of Odysseus both perish by a violent death under luckless circumstances, and their hapless ghosts are alike introduced as suffering some special discomfort in the Underworld. Says the ghost of Patroklos ;—' Bury me with all speed, that I pass the gates of Aïdês. Far off the spirits banish me, nor suffer me to mingle with them beyond the River, but vainly I wander along the wide-gated dwelling of Aïdês.'[5] And, similarly, the ghost of Elpênôr, to whom the last rites had not yet been paid, was wandering woefully on the confines of the dark realm, and prays that his body may not be abandoned ' unwept and unburied.' With the imita-

---

sonages, and the scene of the contest supply the chief clues to the nature of the underlying fact. *E.g.*, the non-Aryan Oriôn is opposed in various ways by Aryan divinities, and slain by Artemis (*Od.* v. 123-4). In an instance such as this both features are blended, but the attack upon Sidê is purely a matter of race and cult.

[1] *Joshua*, xix. 28. The Assyrian Zidunnu-rabu.
[2] *Joshua*, xix. 29. As. Zurra.   [3] Ezekiel, xxviii. 12.
[4] Isaiah, xiv. 15.   [5] *Il.* xxiii. 71-4.

tions and explanations of Vergil, and the folk-lore
aspect of the matter I am not here concerned; but it
is very noticeable that Heabani the friend and comrade in adventure of Izdubar, also died by a violent
death under some almost unknown but very luckless
circumstances,[1] which occasioned him special discomfort in the Underworld. Speaking of *The Twelfth
Izdubar Legend*, Mr. Boscawen observes that it
' relates to the state of the soul of Heabani, which
had been shut out of heaven, owing to the strange
circumstances of his death.'[2] The poet says;—

'To happiness (thou art not admitted).
A pure dress (thou dost not wear).
An onset on earth thou dost not make.
The enfolding of the earth has taken thee.
O Darkness! O Darkness! Mother Ninazu,[3] O Darkness!
Her mighty power as a garment covers thee;'

just as Elpênôr, 'fleeter on foot' than Odysseus in his
ship—for 'the dead ride fast'—came 'beneath the
murky gloom.'[4]

' The resting place of Nergal the unconquered, did not take him,
The earth took him.
Heabani to rest was not admitted.'

The Tablet is much broken, but it seems that the

---

[1] ' After this happened the violent death of Heabani, which added
to the misfortunes of Izdubar; but no fragment of this part of the story
is preserved ' (*C. A. G.* 257).

[2] *Records of the Past*, ix. 129.

[3] *I.e.*, ' Wise-lady-of-the-waters,' a name of Ninkigal (vide *sup.* p. 121).
Nin (cf. Nin-os) means ' lord ' or ' lady ' according to the context; so
we find Ninazu as also a name of the god Hea.

[4] *Od.* xi. 57. It is to be noticed that *zophos*, like *erebos*, particularly
signifies the *western* gloom, and is sometimes simply used for the west as
the dark quarter, *e.g.* Ἤδη γὰρ φάος οἴχεθ' ὑπὸ ζόφον (*Ibid.* iii. 335).

ghost of Heabani is raised by means of an incantation ; and as the story concludes with an account of the joyful state of the spirit of a warrior in the unseen world, we may conclude that Heabani, like Patroklos and Elpênôr, was ultimately enabled to join his fellow shades under satisfactory conditions.

II. *The Sons of Lêda.* Teirêsias, the head of the starry Signs, comes and goes after revealing to the hero his destiny and guiding him by wise counsel ; and as the shades of the bevy of fair women pass before Odysseus, we have a very curious account of the sons of Lêda, ' Kastôr tamer of steeds, and Poly-deukês. These twain yet live but the quickening earth is over them ; and even in the nether world (νέρθεν γῆς—' beneath the earth ') they have honour at the hand of Zeus. And they possess their life in turn, living one day and dying the next, and they have gotten worship even as the gods.' [1] The Aryan origin of the Dioskouroi, whom Herodotos says came to the Hellenes from the Pelasgoi,[2] is clear ;[3] so when Helenê cannot find them amongst the Achaian host, the poet says, 'Them the life-giving earth held fast in Lakedaimôn, in their dear native land.'[4] In one point of view they are thus simply two Hellenik heroes, but at an early period they became curiously connected with the great non-Aryan and adopted astronomical system. The third Euphratean zodiacal

---

[1] *Od.* xi. 300-4.   [2] Vide R. B. Jr., *G. D. M.* i. 176.

[3] 'The twin Asvins or steeds, who represent the Dioskouroi' (Sir G. W. Cox, *Mythology of the Aryan Nations,* 234).

[4] *Il.* iii. 243-4.

Sign is Kas ('The Twins'[1]), and the archaic kosmogonic myth or legend attached to the month is that
of the Two Hostile Brethren (Sun and Moon, Lion
and Unicorn,[2] Nannaros[3]-Sin[4] and Parsondas[5]-Adar-
Sandan-Samas) and the Building of the First City,
i.e., the Universe built up out of chaos in kosmic
order by the Two Great Lights.[6] These 'Great Twin
Brethren'[7] are reduplicated in the two bright stars
of the constellation *Didymoi*, and the Dioskouroi are
their obvious Aryan analogues; so that in the adjust-
ment of divinities to a foreign astrological system[8]
these two became *Gemini*, 'fratres Helenae, lucida
sidera.'[9] So Hyginus says of *Gemini*, 'Hos complures
astrologi Castorem et Pollucem esse dixerunt.'[10] The
rather obscure Homerik account thus at once becomes
most lucid; we see how 'these twain' (Sun and

[1] Cf. Horace: 'geminus Pollux' (*Carmina*, III. xxix. 64).

[2] Vide R. B. Jr., *U.*

[3] As. Nannaru ('the Brilliant') *i.e.*, the Moon.

[4] The Moon-god, Ak. Zu-ên ('Eye-lord'); cf. Mount Sinai.

[5] A variant form of an original which probably also supplied the
name Perseus (vide R. B. Jr., *U.* 54).

[6] Vide R. B. Jr., *L. K. O.* sec. xii. *Gemini.*

[7] As to the Asvins, vide inter al. Bergaigne, *La Religion Védique*,
1883, ii. 431 *et seq.*

[8] The corresponding process in Kem can be more clearly traced by
means of the late Zodiacs of Greek and Roman times. There the solar
god Shu ('Light'), the kosmogonic solar force (Pierret), kosmic heat
and light principle (Tiele), or air (sunlit-air?, Renouf), and the goddess
Tefnut ('Humidity'), the force of solar light (Pierret), heated kosmic
water (Tiele) or dew (Renouf), 'the two Lion-gods,' became the *Gemini*
of Roman times.

[9] Horace, *Carmina*, I. iii. 2. Helenê is considered by many mythologists to be a variant of the Vedic Saramâ, a dawn-name. 'Les
Açvins semblent être avant tout des divinités matinales' (Bergaigne).

[10] *Poeticon Astronomicon*, ii. In voc.

Moon) yet live although the earth is over them, and the earth is 'quickening' in the sense that it constantly produces all the heavenly bodies, even as the Kemic Upper-heaven (Nut) is female for the same reason. That the twain ' have honour at the hand of Zeus,' and 'have gotten worship even as the gods,' is obvious ; and the remaining point is that they ' possess their life in turn, living one day and dying the next.' Now it is equally clear that they ' possess their life in turn,' according to the relation of day and night ; but the poet speaks of them as living together and dying together which presents an apparent difficulty.

The Signs of the Zodiac have been divided for very many ages into diurnal and nocturnal constellations ; the underlying reason for this arrangement had utterly faded away perhaps 3,000 years ago, but it is simply that six of the Signs were originally reduplications of prior diurnal types, and the remaining six of prior nocturnal types. *Gemini* is a diurnal type ; the Sun and Moon are only seen together by day, and in this aspect as the Twins they live and die together ; for should one disappear and the other remain, the latter ceases to be a twin brother and passes into some other mythological phase. When the already familiar mythological aspects of the simpler phenomena of heaven came to be applied to the twelve natural divisions of the then newly-discovered zodiacal cincture, the third division as containing a special pair of bright stars would be a most suitable reduplication of the archaic Twins ; just as in the adjoining constellation *Cancer*—the Crab (or some such creature) being a type of Darkness—we find no specially bright stars, so much so that this Sign has been often called ' the Dark Constellation.' Nor was a further and more purely astronomical reason wanting to justify the choice, for, as Pliny notes, ' Lunam bis coitum cum Sole et in nullo alio signo facere quam Geminis,'[1] an incident which doubtless did not escape the lynx-eye of archaic observation.[2] And this diurnal character of *Gemini* seems even to linger in the Homerik account, inasmuch as it is not seen by Odysseus in the Scheôl-night-world but only referred to.

It is well to notice here a point in Homerik criticism ; the whole of the *Nekyia* has been ' suspected,' and various parts of it have been strongly suspected and that from ancient times. As the early critic was wholly ignorant of the archaic period, his suspicions are not generally very noteworthy ;[3] but the modern critic demands more serious attention,[4] and may be fairly represented in the matter by Dr.

---

[1] *Hist. Nat.* ii. 15.

[2] For treatment of the Law of Reduplication in connexion with the constellation-figures, vide R. B. Jr., *L. K. O.* and *E.* The Diurnal Signs of the Zodiac are the Ram-sun (*Aries*), Sun and Moon (*Gemini*), the Lion-sun (*Leo*), the Holy-sun (*Ara,* now the comparatively modern *Libra*), the Archer-sun (*Sagittarius,* an excellent representation of whom has been very recently found at Sippara-Sepharvaim, ' the city of the Sun '), and the Rain-giving-sun (*Aquarius,* = the Aryan Indra).

[3] Vide *sup.* p. 125.

[4] It will be remembered that I am treating of concept, not of linguistic.

Hayman, who thinks that, *e.g.*, the account of Kastôr
and Polydeukês has been tampered with, 'still, any
such tampering is probably older than Pindar. . .
Some nature-myth, of the alternation of the life and
death of the vegetable world, is probably at the root
of part of the legend.'[1] Whether the root of the
legend is a vegetable one, the reader must judge.
Dr. Hayman does not assist the formation of a conclusion by any specific vegetable suggestions, but
recurs to the matter in an Appendix in which having
restated his ' suspicion ' of the passage, he observes;—
' I can only give as the common ground for this
distrust the wide distance between such mythological
refinements and the simple forms of early legend
which are characteristically Homeric. It is impossible, I should think, to read even the legends
contained in the νεκυία only without feeling this.'
On such a text a long sermon might easily be
preached, suffice it however to ask,—(1) Is a 'mythological refinement' necessarily comparatively modern?
and (2) Is not the idea in the passage a very simple
and natural one ? I think so, and that taken alone it
might justly be regarded as being highly archaic.
Of course when we add the Euphratean connexion of
the whole episode this very reasonable possibility
develops into an almost absolute certainty. We
need not concern ourselves with difficult enquiries
into the exact period of the rise of the later Hellenik
developments of hero-worship, or of any local cult of

[1] *The Odyssey of Homer*, ii. 211.

the Dioskouroi at Lakedaimôn or elsewhere. The Dioskouroi-Asvins on the one hand, and the Euphratean Twins on the other, will reach back to a period far more archaic than can be required by *any* theory of the Homerik poems.

Next as to ' mythological refinements.' I venture to affirm that archaic ideas in their second or perhaps third stage, are often remarkably distinguished by complexity and elaboration ; and am content to leave the decision of this question to students of Vedic and Kemic divinities. But let us turn for an example to the distant field of Polynesian mythology, and notice the kosmogonic scheme of the people of Mangaia, an island in the Hervey Group. The Universe (Avaiki), pictured as a cocoa-nut shell, rests on a stem which tapers to a point; and this point is personified as a demon of unhuman form named Teakaiaroê (' Root-of-all-existence '). At the bottom of the shell is an old woman called Varimatetakave (' the Beginning-and-the-bottom '), and her son Vatea (' Noon ') was the first man. He ' had two magnificent eyes, rarely visible at the same time '—Gemini-Dioskouroi ; they ' possess their life in turn,' and well may Prof. Max Müller say that here there is ' much that will startle those who think that metaphysical conceptions are incompatible with downright savagery.' [1]

III. *The Sons of Iphimedeia.* These famous pair of twins Ôtos, the Vedic Vata (' the Wind '), and

---

[1] *Introduction to the Science of Religion,* 2nd edit. 1882, p. 259 ; vide Gill, *Myths and Songs from the South Pacific.*

Ephialtês ('the On-leaper,' *i.e.* the hurricane), are
children of Poseidôn; whilst their mother's name is
merely a variant intensive of Mêdeia,[1] and she is a
personage 'entirely detached from Hellenic associations.'[2] Thus she is represented as being a votary of
Dionysos.[3] In this account, as in so many, we have
an intermixture of Aryan and non-Aryan myth and
legend; thus the names of the gigantic brethren and
their singular triumph over Arês whom they bound
and imprisoned,[4] embody the Aryan portion of the
myth, being the contest of clouds, hurricane, wind
etc.[5] Their gigantic size is equally Aryan and non-
Aryan; but their connexion with Oriôn, to whom
alone of men they were inferior, their determination
to attack 'the immortals in Olympos,' their effort to
make 'a pathway to the sky,' and their consequent
destruction by the Aryan Apollôn,[6] point to a non-
Aryan element in the story, for Wind and Hurricane
require no such pathway nor do they pile mountain
on mountain to make it. We cannot but remember
the *Legend of the Tower of Babel*,[7] in the building of
which the archaic king Etana[8] seems to have been
concerned;[9] how

'Babylon corruptly to sin went and
    Small and great mingled on the mound;'

---

[1] Vide *sup.* p. 28; cf. Memnôn and Aga-memnôn. As to Memnôn,
Dr. Oppert observes, 'It is possible that *Umman Amman* "house of the
god Amman," was corrupted by the Greeks to Memnonian, the great
edifice of Susa' (*Records of the Past*, vii. 83).

[2] Gladstone, *Homeric Synchronism*, 218.   [3] Diodoros, v. 50.
[4] *Il.* v. 385-91.   [5] Vide R. B. Jr., *E.* 19.   [6] *Od.* xi. 305-20.
[7] Ap. W. St. Chad Boscawen, in *Records of the Past*, vii. 129 *et seq.*
[8] Vide *sup.* p. 114.   [9] Vide *C. A. G.* 103.

until the Divinity

> ' Of their stronghold in the night
> Entirely an end he made,
> In his anger also the secret counsel he poured out ;
> To scatter (abroad) his face he set ;
> He gave a command to make hostile their counsel ; [1]
> Their progress he impeded.' [2]

Much might be added on this subject, and much more will yet be discovered ; suffice it now to indicate an outline, and the presence of Euphratean influence.

The number 9, so frequent in Homerik incident, is prominently introduced in the legend of the sons of Iphimedeia. 'At 9 seasons old they were of breadth 9 cubits, and 9 fathoms in height.' This connexion is Aryan, and the number reappears similarly in Hesiod, *e.g.*, in the 9 years' banishment of the divinity who broke an oath by the water of Styx, in the 9 days fall of the *akmôn*, and in the number of the Muses. Again, to turn to Norse mythology, in the Ragnarok-contest Thorr, suffocated by the floods of venom from the Midhgardhsormr, staggers back 9 paces to show that he ceases to exist in any of the 9 worlds, whilst Heimdallr is styled son of 9 mothers, to show that his influence extends throughout all the worlds. We find these 9 worlds, a reduplication of a prior theory of 3 worlds (heaven, earth and the

---

[1] Or 'to make strange their speech.'

[2] The Tablet is sadly broken, but further and fuller accounts will probably be recovered. The references to the legend in Alexander Polyhistor and Abydênos are familiar.

invisible world, or heaven, atmosphere and earth) referred to in the Vedic Hymns.[1]

IV. *Minôs.* From legend we pass on to sights actually beheld by Odysseus, who on the edge of the Two Worlds, might apply to himself the words of the Kemic votary of Asar (Osiris) :—

' It is I who know the roads of Nu.[2]
The gites of heaven open. The gates of earth open to me.
Seb[3] has opened the bolts, he has opened the lower abode wile.[4]
I am the Sun who proceeds from Nu.
I am the orb, what I hate is repose.[5]
The great Soul[6] has come along the noble road.
I stand at the earth as Seb.[7]
The holder of the secrets of the Gate at the Balance of the Sun,
Who places the Feather in it daily.[8]
The sceptre in the front of Seb in that Balance of the Sun.
He places Truth in it daily.[9]

That is to say, the Sun has turned back to the earth on his downward evening course, and has reached the western horizon-gateway. Here at the abode of Seb,

----

[1] ' Il est maintenant établi que l'univers a été divisé par les Rishis en six, sept, *neuf,* ou vingt et un ' (Bergaigne, *La Religion Védique,* ii. 129). Probably the prominence of the number 9 is also connected with the 9 Moons of gestation.

[2] The Firmament.

[3] The time-measuring Earth-god, Time being marked by the passage of the heavenly bodies through the Gates of Hades, eastern and western.

[4] *Funereal Ritual,* lxviii.

[5]
      ' It little profits that an idle king,
      . . . . . I mete and dole
      Unequal laws unto a savage race.
      I cannot rest from travel . . . .
          I am become a name ;
      . . always roaming with a hungry heart '
               (Tennyson, *Ulysses*).

[6] The Sun. [7] *Funereal Ritual,* lxxxv.
[8] *Ibid.* xii. [9] *Ibid.* cxx.

lord of the horizon-gate, he holds the secrets of the Underworld, into which he sees and is about to descend. ' The Balance of the Sun ' [1] is the Sun himself, ' the Lord of the Two Worlds,' [2] poised at the horizon between the Upper and the Underworld. The ' Feather ' which he places in it daily, and which is also called ' Truth,' is his own revealing solar eye. [3] This is the position of Odysseus by the trench.

The shades of the Achaian heroes having departed, Odysseus next ' saw Minos, glorious son of Zeus, wielding a golden sceptre, giving sentence from his throne to the dead, while they sat and stood around the prince, asking his dooms through the wide-gated house of Aïdês.' [4] Minôs ' appears in Homer as the greatest and most important of his archaic personages : ' [5] and has a triple aspect, as connected alike with Aryan and Semitic mythology, and also as representing to some extent a genuine historical tradition. His Phoenician connexion has been fully illustrated ; [6] he is the son of Europê (Ereb, ' the West ')

---

[1] Achilleus Tatios says that ' the substitution of Libra for the Claw of the Scorpion was imported from Egypt' (Prof. Sayce, in *T.* iii. 149); and the zodiacal *Balance*, the only Sign of the Twelve which is not Euphratean in origin, and which has been said to mark ' the equality of the days and nights at the equinoxes,' appears to be a reduplication of this balance of the horizon-sun. It is found, as of course, on the late Kemic Zodiacs.　　　　　　　　[2] *Funereal Ritual,* xcv.

[3] So of the two Plumes of Har (Horos), the youthful Sun-god, it is said ;—' His eyes are the plumes on his head' (*Ibid.* cap. xvii.), the god being provided with an eye for Northern and an eye for Southern Kem.

[4] *Od.* xi. 568-71.　　　　　[5] Gladstone, *Juventus Mundi,* 118.

[6] *Ibid.* 118-22; *Homeric Synchronism,* 213; R. B. Jr., *G. D. M.* i. 38; ii. 142.

daughter of Phoinix or of Agênôr ('the Lordly'),
king of Phoinikia, whose name is merely a translation
of Baal, and who is styled a twin-brother of Bêlos ;
but his name is Aryan, the Indian Manu, Man as the
'measurer' and 'thinker.' Like Aiêtês and Atlas he
is 'baleful,'[1] for dread and terrible is his might, and
man must die ere he stand before the judgment-seat ;
he is also a sterner and darker reduplication of the
Sun-god in his character of the Dian-nisi ('Judge-of-
men'), his brother Rhadamanthos, the Kemic Rhota-
menti ('Judge-of-the-Hidden-world'), being a milder
and brighter reduplication of the same august personage. The Sun-god, alike in the theory of Nile
and Euphrates, has committed to him the great task
of judging mortals in the Unseen-world ; and the
name and alleged wisdom and law-giving character of
Minôs are based upon this idea. So an Akkadian
Hymn invokes the 'Spirit of Udu, king of justice,'[2]
Ud, Ut, or *Udu* being a name of the Akkadian Sun-
god, and the Assyrian translation reading Samas.[3] So
an Inscription of Nabukuduruzur the Great states :—

'To the Sun, the Judge supreme, the temple of Dian-nisi,
His temple in Bab-ilu grandly I built.'[4]

[1] *Od.* xi. 322 ; vide *sup.* p. 35.   [2] Lenormant, *Chaldean Magic*, 17.
[3] Heb. Shemesh. The Ak. *ud* means 'sun, day, eye, dawn, light,
white,' and 'to rise,' and *zal*, As. *samsu*, is another name of the sun.
Ud-zal, ('Rising-sun') recalls the Etruscan Usil, with respect to which
Dr. Is. Taylor observes ;—'Hesychius says that among the Etruscans
ausel meant the "dawn." We may conclude, therefore, that the USIL
of the monuments personified the "rising sun"' (*Etruscan Researches*,
143). The reverse of the *templum* of Piacenza (Vide Deecke, *Etruskische
Forschungen*, Das Templum von Piacenza, Pl. III.) shows two circular
divisions, one Usils—that of the Sun, and the other Tivs—that of the
Moon.   [4] Vide *T.* ii. 32.

The 'golden sceptre' or wand of light-gods marks a reminiscence of actual radiation.[1]

V. *Oriôn.* Next, says Odysseus, 'I marked the great Orion driving the wild beasts together over the mead of asphodel, the very beasts which he himself had slain on the lonely hills, with a strong mace all of bronze in his hands, that is ever unbroken.'[2] That very remarkable and thoroughly Euphratean personage Oriôn is most appropriately encountered in the Eleventh Odyssey ; and, as I have elsewhere discussed the Oriôn-myth, alike in its primary solar and in its reduplicated constellational character, at some length, I will only notice it briefly here and refer the reader to my previous remarks.[3] Now, as Oriôn is also a constellation, identical with the Euphratean constellation Dumuzi (Tammuz), and as we have in this vision of Odysseus a combination of Night and Death, let me refer to a remarkable statement of Diodoros, in his brief *résumé* of the Chaldean astronomico-astrology of his day.[4] Having stated the Chaldean scheme of 36 stars or constellations, 12 northern, 12 zodiacal and 12 southern, he says ;—' And of these those which are visible they reckon as belonging to the living, τοὺς δ' ἀφανεῖς, τοῖς τετελευτηκόσιν προσωρίσθαι νομίζουσιν.[5] Here, then, is independent testimony

---

[1] For Aryan illustration of the concept of Minôs, and his being slain in the West by Kokalos, the Night-gloom, vide Sir G. W. Cox, *Mythology of the Aryan Nations*, 328-9.

[2] *Od.* xi. 572-4.

[3] Vide R. B. Jr., *G. D. M.* ii. 270 *et seq.* ; *E.* sec. iv.

[4] For a general examination of the passage, vide *E.* sec. xxvii.

[5] Diodoros, ii. 31.

relative to the Euphratean theory of constellations in the world of the dead, a line of thought which certainly much assists in explaining the sights seen by the hero, and confirms the view here put forth of the connexion between Night and the Shade-world. But Oriôn is also solar, and as such was beloved by Eôs and slain by the lunar Artemis; [1] and that the Sun should shine among the dead is an idea familiar to the Homerik poet as to bards of Akkad and of Kem. So Hêlios threatens;—'If they pay me not full atonement for the cattle, I will go down to Aïdês and shine among the dead.' [2] The poet states that the Oriôn-sun drives triumphantly through the Underworld the beasts which he had slain 'on the lonely hills' of heaven in the Upperworld; he still pursues the endless chase, and especially follows with his Dogs the Hare-moon. The heavenly hills are lonely because the solar hero is ever, or very frequently and naturally, regarded as being alone. He has indeed sailors with him in his solar barque, but generally, like Dionysos, he 'wanders abroad through the boundless Olympos,' the lonely Bellerophôn, the unattended Oriôn, Melqarth who hunts by himself, Dumuzi the 'Only son' of heaven. The poet styles Oriôn πελώριον, 'portentous;' and in his stellar aspect as the head of the Southern Signs, [3] he burns on high a fate-revealer and a mighty Sign for evermore. In his

---

[1] *Od.* v. 121–4.

[2] *Ibid.* xii. 382–3. For comment on this passage, vide R. B. Jr., *G. D. M.* i. 392–3.

[3] *Il.* xviii. 486–8.

solar aspect he is slain by the Scorpion of Darkness,[1] which is reduplicated in the zodiacal *Scorpio*.[2] The Ak. *ur*, 'light,' As. *uru*, Heb. *aor*, reappears in the Boiotik Urion,[3] Aorion, Oarion.[4]

In the occult legend of the god Zu ('the Wise,' 'the Giver'), we find that 'the tablets of destiny, stolen by Zu, for the benefit, apparently, of mankind, formed the vault of the palace of the under-world.'[5] We read :—

> 'The tablets of doom his hand took,
> The attributes of Bel he seized, he laid hold of the oracles.
> Zu fled away and a rugged mountain concealed (him).
> He spread darkness.'

Now here we have another curious illustration of the

---

[1] Apollodoros, I. iv. 3; Servius, *Aeneid*, i. 539; Ovid, *Fasti*, v. 541-3.

[2] Vide R. B. Jr., *L. K. O.* sec. xvii.

[3] 'Hunc Hyrieus, quia sic genitus, vocat Uriona' (Ovid, *Fasti*, v. 535); Hyginus, *Poeticon Astronomicon*, ii. 34; Schol. in Germanicus, Latin version of the *Phainomena* of Aratos, in voc.

[4] Korinna, *Fragment* ii. 'She represented Orion as a noble and pious man, a civilizer of the barbarous country' (K. O. Müller, *Introduction to a Scientific System of Mythology*, 347), the usual *rôle* of the Sun-god. So Pindar speaks of φύσιν 'Ωαριωνείαν (*Isth.* iii. 67), and the idea of gigantic stature, sun as against stars, is conspicuous throughout the myth. Steinthal remarks that 'the formation of proper names of men and places by the termination *ôn* is excessively common' (In Goldziher, *Mythology among the Hebrews*, 408, note), and instances Dâg-ôn and Shimsh-ôn. I think that this *ôn* probably often represents the Ak. *an*, *ana*, *anna*, 'high, sky, god.' Thus Dagôn, called by Berosos Ôdakôn (*Chaldaika*, ii. Fragment 6), = the Ak. Udukana ('the Lord-who-rises-high'); and being the Fish-sun (*Piscis*, afterwards *Pisces*) becomes almost necessarily connected with the Semitic *dâg*, 'fish.' Oriôn similarly = Ur-ana ('the Light-of-heaven'). So Orchamus, 'septimus a prisco numeratur origine Belo' (Ovid, *Metam.* iv. 212-3), = Ur-kamu ('Burning-light.' Cf. Shakspere, 'You ever-burning lights above,' *Othello*, iii. 3).

[5] *C. A. G.* 116.

intimate connexion between the Underworld and the Night-sky. For, I think, it is the stellar 'tablets of destiny,' which of course are the rightful property of the Heaven-sire, that this Akkadian Promêtheus and darkness-spreader lays unholy hands upon; and so 'Nabu, the powerful,' who is primarily 'the meridian sun,' is commanded to '(slay) Zu with his weapon.' Hence the very close link between 'the vault of the palace of the under-world,' the cave of Kalypsô, and the palace of Kirkê.

VI. *Tityos.* Next seen was 'Tityos, son of Earth, lying on a levelled ground, outstretched over 9 roods' length, and vultures twain beset him one on either side, and gnawed at his liver, piercing even to the caul, but he drave them not away with his hands. For he had dealt violently with Leto, the famous bedfellow of Zeus, as she went up to Pytho through the fair lawns of Panopeus.'[1] The other Homerik reference to the giant states how the Phaiakes 'carried Rhadamanthos, of the fair hair, to visit Tityos, son of Earth' in Euboia. 'Even thither they went, and accomplished the journey on the self-same day.'[2] The acute student of archaic myths will, I think, unhesitatingly conclude that we have here something genuine and occult, something the meaning of which had long been forgotten, whilst the form of its expression remained fossilized. Ephoros, B.C. 340, in his *Historiai*[3] tells us Euemeristically that Tityos, βίαιον ἄνδρα καὶ παράνομον, was slain by Apollôn

[1] *Od.* xi. 576–81.   [2] *Ibid.* vii. 323–6.   [3] *Fragment* lxx.

(=Rhadamanthos [1]); and we have seen [2] what was the nature of his offence with respect to Lêtô. Now this visitation of Tityos by Rhadamanthos was evidently judicial; [3] as Dionysos the solar judge, he is carried in a day by the Phaiakian ship of cloud-land [4] to Euboia, not the historical and geographical island, but the country of the Good-ox. The special coin-type of the island of Euboia is the head-of-an-ox, or an ox *statant*; [5] and on it was the cave called Boös Aulê where Iô was said to have brought forth Epaphos. [6] The ancients supposed that it had been severed from Boiôtia ('Ox-land') by an earthquake, and the name has reference to the wondrous ox or cow of Kadmos ('the Easterner'=the Sun), marked with the full moon, [7] and which led Kadmos through Phokis, the coins of which bear the head of an ox and also the heads of three oxen placed triangularly, [8] and

---

[1] Vide *sup.* p. 145.   [2] *Sup.* p. 132.

[3] 'The sense of ἐφοράω in H. is to "visit or oversee for punishment"' (Hayman, *The Odyssey of Homer*, ii. 25).

[4] Vide Sir G. W. Cox, *Mythology of the Aryan Nations*, 487 *et seq.* That actual non-Aryan and historical traits are shown in the portraiture of Alkinoös and his people is obvious, but the Natural Phenomena element is there also.

[5] 'Qui typi ad nomen insulae adludunt' (Eckhel, *Doctrina Numorum Veterum*, ii. 322).

[6] Strabo, X. i. 3.

[7] 'It had on each of its sides a white mark, like the circle of the moon when full' (Pausanias, IX. xii. 1). 'It had on each side a mark like the moon' (Schol. in Aristophanes, *Batrachoi*, 1256).

[8] If the reader will refer to R. B. Jr., *U.* sec. ix., he will see the lunar origin of the Triquetra, a name actually applied by the Roman poets to Sicily, which as Triuacria was early identified with the Homerik Thrinakiê (*Od.* xi. 107), 'the Three-pointed,' a name which does not refer to the *thrinax* or trident of Poseidôn, but to the points of the three crescent-moons surrounding the full-moon. It is almost unnecessary to

at length lay down on the site of Thebai.[1] This lunar
cow, ox, or bull, reduplicated in the constellation
Taurus, 'the exaltation of the Moon,'[2] leads on the
Sun into the moon-land (Euboia, Boiôtia),[3] where he
judges and sentences the offending Tityos. It takes
but one day to reach the distant Euboia and to return. Rhadamanthos is, of course, a variant phase of
Minôs.

The attack on Lêtô is said to have taken place

Πυθῶδ' ἐρχομένην διὰ καλλιχόρου Πανοπῆος.

She was going to Pythô, a name for that part of
Phokis at the foot[4] of Parnassos; and Pausanias

say that the Homerik poet knows nothing about Sicily and never refers
to it. Thus Mr. Gladstone, in his Homerik map, places the island of
Thrinakiê in the north-east.

[1] 'The Ox is called *Theba* among the Syrians' (*Etymol. Magnum,* in
voc. *Theba*; cf. Schol. in Lykophrón, 1206).

[2] Porphyry, *Peri tou en Od. tôn Nymph. Ant.* viii.

[3] Selênê is styled Taurokerôs (*Pseudo-Orphik Hymn,* ix. 2), and
Pausanias describes her statue at Elis, καὶ τῆς μὲν κέρατα ἐκ τῆς κεφαλῆς
(*Periêgêsis,* VI. xxiv. 5). According to Olympiodôros, 'the ancient
theologists' said that 'the moon is drawn by two bulls' (*MS. Comment.*
on the *Gorgias* of Platón), and the moon-car, bearing a crescent and thus
drawn, is given by Lajard from an Asiatic original (*Culte de Mithra,*
Pl. lxvii. Fig. 8). An ox-drawn moon-car is also depicted in the MS. of
Cicero's Translation of Aratos. Of the lunar Astarté (Istar, afterwards
planetary) we read, ἡ δὲ 'Αστάρτη ἐπέθηκε τῇ ἰδίᾳ κεφαλῇ βασιλείας
παράσημον κεφαλὴν ταύρου (Sanchouniathón, i. 7); and she appears on
coins cow-headed or bull-headed accordingly. Similarly, Istar sends
'the Bull of heaven' ('It was a constellation, perhaps Taurus,' Prof.
Sayce, *C. A. G.* 231) against the solar Izdubar.

[4] The name Pythô or Pythón probably = 'informateur' (Lenormant,
La Divination, 161). 'Une troisième opinion, assez en faveur, dérive Πυθώ
de βῦθος = *gouffre* (angl. *bottom*).' Or, again, 'Python n'est peut-être
qu'un Typhon à peine défiguré' (Bouché-Leclercq, *Histoire de la Divination,* iii. 65, note). Plutarch says;—'It is far from quiet or orderly
work, when souls, separated from mind, get possession of a body subject
to passions. Of such souls came perchance the Tityi and the Typhons,

understood the latter half of the line differently from
Messrs. Butcher and Lang. He says ;—' I was not
able to conjecture why Homer called Panopeus *kalli-
choros*, until I learnt the reason from the Athenians
who are called Thyades. The Thyades are Attik
women who come to Parnassos yearly, and they and
the Delphik women celebrate orgies to Dionysos.
The Thyades are wont to form dances (χοροὺς) on
the way from Athens, both elsewhere and amongst
the Panopeans. Therefore the epithet applied by
Homer to Panopeus seems to indicate the dance of
the Thyades.'[1] Now in the universal Dionysiak
nature-dance, of which I have treated elsewhere,[2] the
stars bear an important part. Even the Moon and
the 50 daughters of Nêreus who are in the sea,
celebrate in choric dance Dêmêtêr and Persephonê,
which dance is led off by 'the starry-faced ether of
Zeus;'[3] the protagonists in 'the chorus of stars,' as
Maximus Tyrius[4] calls it, being the Pleïades.[5] These

and that Typhon [Python?] who used to hinder and trouble the oracular
power at Delphi' (*On the Face in the Moon's Orb*, xxx., ap. C. W. King).
For the connexion between the monster Typhâôn and Pythô, vide
Homerik Hymn *Eis Apollôna*, 349 *et seq.* Teb, the Kemic name of the
hippopotamus, supplies a town-name and also the name Tebhu, the god
of Teb, *i.e.*, Set, whom the Hellenes called Typhon; according to Tiele,
'the Greeks must have got the name Typhon from the Phoenicians, who
identified Set tebhu with their god of storms, *Ziphon*' (*Hist. of the
Egyptian Religion*, 51, note 3). Pythô = 'the Oracle' (Sayce).

[1] Pausanias, X. iv. 1, 2; vide R. B. Jr., *G. D. M.* i. 271-2; cf. the
sacred spring of Dêmêtêr at Eleusis, called Kallichorôs ('the Fount-of-
the-beauteous-dance'), Homerik Hymn *Eis Demêtran*, 273; Pausanias,
l. xxxviii. 5.

[2] Vide *G. D. M.* i. 103 *et seq.*   [3] Euripides, *Iôn*, 1074 *et seq.*

[4] *Dialexeis*, xiv.; cf. Manethô, v. 7.

[5] Vide Hyginus, *Poeticon Astronomicon*, ii. 21.

' ethereal dances of the stars ' [1] are imitated by earthly
votaries; for a great part of archaic ritual originates
in an imitation more or less exact of natural phenomena. Panopeus ('the All-seeing') is a variant of
Argos Panoptês,[2] and a son of Asteropeia; even
whilst yet unborn he quarrelled with his brother
Krisos (the solar ' Judge'). As Lêtô (the Holy-
darkness) was passing through the beautiful stellar
dancers, she was attacked by Tityos ('the Extended'),
the starry host regarded as a vast night-vanquishing
giant, stretched out 9 roods, *i.e.*, over the whole
heaven-vault; and this profanation was, as of course,
avenged by Apollôn or Rhadamanthos; or, again,
by ' the swift-winged dart of Artemis,' [3] as the star-
quelling Moon. At Delphoi the mother and her two
glorious children, Apollôn and Artemis, were all
three represented piercing the vanquished Tityos
with their arrows.[4]

The remaining point in the myth is that (1) vultures
twain beset the giant, (2) one on either side, but (3) he
did not drive them away with his hands, although he
is not stated to have been bound. In mythological
artistic combinations when two personages, creatures,
or other objects, stand one on each side of a central
object or design, they very frequently represent the
powers of morning and evening, *e.g.*, dawn and
twilight, the rising and setting sun, darkness eastern

---

[1] Euripides, *Elektra*, 467.

[2] An individual Panopeus is named by Homer as the sire of Epeios,
the boxer (*Il.* xxiii. 665); cf. Pausanias, II. xxix. 4.

[3] Pindar, *Pyth.* iv. 90.   [4] Pausanias, X. xi. 1.

and western, etc. Thus in a Kemic design showing
the Soul rising heavenward from the dead body, it is
guarded and assisted by the Ram-headed-sun[1] eastern
and western. Thus, again, in Euphratean design
the heavenly altar with its solar flame is guarded
or assailed on either side by a Scorpion-darkness-
demon;[2] or the Grove of the Underworld, eastern
and western, is shown by a palm-tree on either side
of a central scene.[3] Now in Euphratean myth we
meet with 'the divine Storm-bird,' 'the divine Zu-
bird' above noticed, who 'spreads darkness;' and
this creature is also known as 'the Giant-bird,' suitable to attack a giant, 'the Bird with the sharp beak,'
'the flesh-eating Bird;'[4] like the Stymphalian birds,
'eaters of human flesh,' warred on and vanquished
by the solar Hêraklês. This Bird of storm and darkness, which has various Aryan analogues, is reduplicated in the Darkness eastern and western. These
flesh-eating Vultures[5] of blackness prey upon the
stellar Tityos, as the Kemic 'Crocodile [Darkness]
of the West fed upon the Achmu Uretu (the setting
stars);' and as the Vultures are two, so the one Crocodile is reduplicated in 'the Crocodiles of the East and
West.'[6] Hence, too, the Vultures beset Tityos 'one
on either side,' a delicate incident bearing convincing

---

[1] *Ba* means both 'soul' and 'ram;' the Sun as the Great-soul
therefore appears at times ram-headed.

[2] Vide R. B. Jr., *E.* Fig. 3; *C. A. G.* Fig. 27.

[3] *Ibid.* Fig. 12.   [4] Vide *E.* 69.

[5] There is no special point in the Birds being called 'vultures;' γύψ
perhaps represents a Kemic term (vide Wharton, *Etyma Graeca*, 40).

[6] Vide R. B. Jr., *E.* Appendix I.

testimony to the truly archaic character of the story. Representations of the human constellation-figures often show them with extended arms; so Aratos says of Andromedê, the Chained-lady;—

> ' And there, too, hath she both her arms outspread,
> With chains upon them e'en in heaven; aloft
> And thus outstretched those hands are ever held.' [1]

So we read ' Canst thou loose the bands of Oriôn?' [2] These figures are, as it were, fastened to the sky with golden nails, and so the bands of Tityos are not mentioned, for his fetters form a part of the Giant himself; and he cannot free his hands to drive away the Birds, whose beaks pierce ' even to the bowels' (δέρτρον ἔσω), *i.e.*, to the very centre (of the sky).

Lastly, the stellar Giant is a reduplication of the simpler solar Giant, Oriôn the Sun and Oriôn the Constellation. This is excellently shown in the instance of the solar Hêraklês. ' He is of many shapes [like the constellations], he devours all things and produces all things, he slays and he heals. Round his head he bears the Morning and the Night, and as living through the hours of darkness he wears a robe of stars (ἀστροχίτων),' [3] and thus becomes Dionysos Nebridopeplos.[4] So arises naturally the idea of a stellar giant, Asterios—whose body measured ten cubits in length,[5] or Asteriôn who married Europê

---

[1] *Phainomena*, 202-4.

[2] *Job*, xxxviii. 31. Whether the constellation *Orion* is referred to or not in the original, is immaterial in this connexion.

[3] Sir G. W. Cox, *Mythology of the Aryan Nations*, 229, note 4.

[4] Vide R. B. Jr., *G. D. M.* ii. 19 *et seq.*; *U.* 76 *et seq.*

[5] Pausanias, I. xxxv. 5.

(the Darkness) and brought up Minôs and Rhada-manthos.[1] The stars may be at peace as well as at war with Darkness. But Tityos has his triumph and revenge; Êôs comes and frees him from his tormen-tors, and his strong hands, bound no longer, grasp and strangle the two Birds,[2] even as the infant Hêraklês slays the two Snakes.

VII. *Tantalos.* Odysseus next 'beheld Tantalos in grievous torment, standing in a mere and the water came nigh unto his chin.' In vain 'that old man,' an expression repeated—he being the head of the family of Pelops—stoops to drink, the water

---

[1] Apollodoros, III. i. 2; Diodoros, iv. 60.

[2] A Euphratean cylinder, given by Creuzer and elsewhere, shows a four-winged divine personage standing between two large Birds whose necks he grasps whilst their mouths are open as if they were being strangled, or at all events severely handled. Another design (Lajard, *Culte de Mithra*, Pl. lxi. Fig. 7) shows an attack by a divine personage on three large birds, a scene repeated on Greek gems showing the contest between Hêraklês and the Stymphalian Birds. The solar Promêtheus (Sk. Pramantha), is tormented in the same way as Tityos until rescued by Hêraklês, and the connexion in idea between the Liver, Space, the Points of the Compass, etc., has received fresh and very suggestive illus-tration from the careful study made by Dr. Deecke of the *Templum* of Piacenza ('Die Leber ein *templum*,' *Etruskische Forschungen und Studien*, Zweites Heft, 1882). Hezekiel (xxi. 21) tells how the king of Babylon when using divination, inspected the liver; and Diodoros (ii. 29) bears testimony to the Kaldean science of interpreting the future from the appearance of the entrails of animals. M. Lenormant has edited a text (*Choix de Textes*, No. 87) which treats of deductions to be drawn from the appearance of the heart of a dog, fox, ram, horse, ox, lion, bear, fish, serpent, and various other creatures (vide Lenormant, *La Divination chez les Chaldéens*, 55); and if the texts treating of the art come fully to light, it will doubtless be possible to arrive at the *rationale* of the system which, like all such ideas, is mainly founded on actual natural incident, anthropomorphic analogy, and synchronous occurrence. The Proto-Aryan *yakan, yakart*, becomes the Sk. *yakrit*, Gk. *hépar*, Lat. *jecur*, Lith. *jekna*, Lett. *aknis*, Bohem. *jatra*, Welsh *iau*.

vanishes and black earth shows at his feet; and when he stretches out his hands in fruitless attempt to clutch pears, apples, figs in the bright grove 'overhead,' 'the wind would toss them to the shadowy clouds.'[1] Archilochos,[2] Alkaios, Alkman,[3] Pindar,[4] and Polygnôtos[5] represent a stone as placed over his head by Zeus and ever ready to crush him. Polygnôtos also portrayed his Homerik sufferings. The solar stone which rolls down again on Sisyphos is the stone which threatens to crush Tantalos; and in each case is a reduplication of the tormented personage, a blending of ideas which in their totality make up a singular anthropomorphic story. These phases of the suffering Sun suitably appear to the hero in the joyless realms of Aïdes. Moral in their origin there is none; the Tantalos-sun, Promêtheus-like, steals the blessings of heaven (food of the gods[6]), or discovers its secrets[7] to men, and must suffer for the offence. As Sir G. W. Cox observes;—'The punishments of Tantalos and Ixiôn [who is referred to by Pindar as being a fourth sufferer with the Homerik three], of Lykâôn and Sisyphos, are involved in the very idea of these beings. The sun, who woos the dawn, yet drives her from him as he rises in the sky. He loves the dew which his rays burn up; and if he shine on the earth too fiercely, its harvests must be withered. If his face approaches the stream too

---

[1] *Od.* xi. 582–92.
[2] *Fragment* liii.
[3] Schol. Pindar, *Olymp.* i. 97.
[4] *Olymp.* i. 90; *Isth.* vii. 21.
[5] Pausanias, X. xxxi. 2.
[6] Pindar, *Olymp.* i. 98.
[7] Diodoros, iv. 74.

closely, the watercourses will soon be beds of gaping slime. The penalty paid by Tantalos is bound up with the phrases which described the action of the sun.'[1]

As to the name Tantalos, we may safely agree with Dr. Hayman that it 'is from an Asiatic source.'[2] Tantalos, the Paphlagonian or Lydian king, whose tomb was shown at Mount Sipylos,[3] is a thoroughly non-Aryan personage, however much Aryan mythological ideas may have twined round him. Diodoros speaks of his being expelled from Paphlagonia by Ilos;[4] and as Taltal is an Akkadian name of the god Hea, we may have here a tradition based upon an early contest between the cults of rival divinities. If to the Akkadian concept of Hea, an archaic Sun-god[5] of the Underworld, we add the Aryan view of solar sufferings, the product is a Tantalos or Taltalos in the gloomy regions of the Shades. Lucretius, not unjustly, ridicules those who credulously believed in the actual sufferings of Tantalos and his fellows, and points out that the only known examples of parallel woes occur on earth, not in an unseen world :—

' Nec miser impendens magnum timet aëre saxum
Tantalus, ut fama est, cassa formidine torpens :
Sed magis in vita divum metus urget inanis
Mortaleis ; casumque timent, quemcunque ferat fors.

---

[1] *Mythology of the Aryan Nations*, 185.

[2] *The Odyssey of Homer*, ii. 241. 'Benfey derives the name from ταλάω by reduplication—τάλταλος, the much-enduring' (Gladstone, *Homeric Synchronism*, 215).

[3] Pausanias, II. xxii. 4; V. xiii. 4. [4] Diodoros, iv. 74.

[5] Vide M. Lenormant 'on the relationship between Hea and Oannes' (*Chaldean Magic*, 201 *et seq.*).

Nec Tityon volucres ineunt Acherunte iacentem ;

. . . .

Sed Tityus nobis hic est, in amore iacentem
Quem volucres lacerant. . .
Sisyphus invita quoque nobis ante oculos est,
Qui petere a populo fasceis saevasque secureis
Imbibit, et semper victus tristisque recedit.'[1]

VIII. *Sisyphos.* This personage, elsewhere described as a ' son of Aiolos ' and the ' craftiest of men,'[2]
is then seen by the hero vainly trying to roll his
' monstrous ($\pi\epsilon\lambda\acute{\omega}\rho\iota\text{o}\nu$[3]) stone' over the hill top.[4] The
solar ' stone which Sisyphos has with huge toil rolled
to the mountain summit (the zenith) must slip from
his grasp and dash down again into the valley below.'[5]
He can never succeed in pushing it over the brow of
the hill, so that it may roll down the *other* or invisible
side of heaven. The complete presentation of a myth
such as that of Sisyphos, would require a separate
monograph, but the result of an analysis of its varied
details will merely confirm the view here maintained. Sisyphos, a king of non-Aryan and oriental
associations, brother of Athamas and Salmôneus,[6] husband of the stellar Meropê and votary of the cult of
Melikertês,[7] is a gold-lover,[8] and a patron of naviga-

---

[1] *De Rerum Natura,* iii. 993 *et seq.*   [2] *Il.* vi. 153–4.
[3] Vide *sup.* p. 63, note 4.
[4] *Od.* xi. 593–600. As to the non-Aryan associations of Sisyphos,
vide Gladstone, *Homeric Synchronism,* 215.
[5] Sir G. W. Cox, *Mythology of the Aryan Nations,* 185.
[6] Vide *sup.* p. 132.   [7] Pausanias, II. i. 3; Apollodoros, III. iv. 3.
[8] No one would suppose that any personage was solar merely from
such a trait, but it becomes very noticeable in the connexion when combined with many other distinctly solar characteristics. The links between gold and solar divinities are endless, and the circumstance supplied

tion.[1] Like Tantalos he betrays the designs of the gods, and reveals their counsels. Perhaps the most interesting legend connected with him is that recorded by Pherekydês[2] the Athenian, which states that Sisyphos bound Thanatos (' Death ') who had been sent to him by Zeus, and who was at length freed by Arês. Sisyphos was then taken to the Underworld, but having previously arranged with his wife Meropê that no funeral rites should be paid him, he obtained permission from Aïdês to return to earth in order to enforce them. Once back again to the light he declined to re-enter the shadowy realm, and having at length died in extreme old age, was made to roll a stone to or in the Underworld as a punishment. This triumph of Sisyphos, whose name is generally and perhaps correctly explained as meaning the 'Very-wise,' over Death and the Underworld, reminds us of the famous victory of Hêraklês over Thanatos, so finely reimmortalized by Browning. For as the Sun-god is the first to die and find out the dread way to the Shades, so is he the first to vanquish them unstained by corruption. Meropê, the dark Pleïad, daughter of Atlas the constant pole, and connected with Merops the Aithiopian

a natural basis for the commercial value of the metal (vide R. B. Jr., *E.* 49, note 4). Dr. Paley has called my attention to the very interesting passage in Pindar (*Isth.* iv. 1–3), where the poet declares that it is through Theia (' the Divine'), the source of light, daughter of Ouranos and Gê (Hesiod, *Theogonia*, 135, 371) and the Μᾶτερ 'Αελίου, that ' men esteem gold beyond other things.'

[1] Like Hêlios, Apollôn, Hêraklês, Chrysôr, Melqarth, Odysseus, Izdubar, Oannês, Ôdakôn, and other solar heroes (vide R. B. Jr., *U.* 19 ; *E.* 12 *et seq.*

[2] *Fragment* lxxviii. ; vide Schol. in *Il.* vi. 153.

king who became the constellational *Eagle*, can kindle
no sufficient funeral pyre in honour of her husband
the departed Sun. Sisyphos ('the Very-wise') may in
his oriental phase (*i.e.*, as unconnected with Aryan
mythology) be, like Tantalos, a variant of Hea, 'god
of wisdom and knowledge,' and ' lord of the deep.'
But such questions as these can only be definitely
settled when far more particulars have been recovered
respecting the vast influence which was undoubtedly
exercised by Euphratean regions upon the whole of
Asia Minor. The burial-place of Sisyphos was secret
and mysterious,[1] a circumstance often connected with
the demise of a solar hero.[2]

IX. *Hêraklês.* The next apparition beheld by
the hero is the phantom of the mighty Hêraklês,
but Hêraklês himself it is expressly stated rejoices
amongst the deathless gods with Hêbê (' Youth ')
as his bride. The genuineness of the passage has been
greatly questioned, and the standpoint of the doubters
has been expressed by Dr. Hayman, as already
noticed.[3] It is obvious that we should require to
have a careful analysis of the so-called ' simple' [that
is, ' simpler'] forms ' of which Dr. Hayman speaks, in
order to enable us to make a proper comparison.
But, apart from this survey, is ' the dichotomy of
one into a phantom and a beatified hero ' an un-
archaic idea, either on general or special grounds?
The instances which I have quoted from the mytho-

---

[1] Pausanias, II. ii. 2.   [2] Vide R. B. Jr., *G. D. M.* ii. 293.
[3] Vide *sup.* p. 138.

logy of Mangaia, and many others that might be cited, dispose of the objection so far as the general question is concerned ; whilst the endless glorious life and daily death of the Sun on his nightly visit to the Underworld supply the strongest possible natural basis for such a dichotomy in the case of a solar hero. And as regards either gods or men, is it necessary to do more than to refer to the almost universal Doctrine of the Double, of which the Kemic Ka,[1] the Iranian Fravashi, and the Akkadian Utuk[2] are special instances ?

Hêraklês appears 'with bow uncased, and shaft upon the string, fiercely glancing around, like one in the act to shoot ;' in fact in the solar aspect of *Sagittarius*, who is thus depicted on a Tablet brought from Sippara, the solar city, and now in the British Museum. The dead around him make a clamour, and are compared to ' fowls flying every way in fear ;' and the whole description recalls the ultimate constellational arrangement in which the arrow of Hêraklês (*Sagitta*) appears in heaven as shot between the Birds (*Cygnus* and *Aquila*).[3] As noticed[4] the

---

[1] Vide P. le Page Renouf, *On the true sense of an important Egyptian Word* (*T.* vi. 494 *et seq.*).

[2] Vide Lenormant, *La Divination*, 153.

[3] Vide R. B. Jr., *E.* sec. xxix. Hêraklês is said to be ἐρεμνῆ ['Ερεμνός = 'Ερεβεννός, ' Of-the-nature-of-Erebos,' setting, chthonian, dark] νυκτὶ ἐοικὼς (*Od.* xi. 606); the Sun is often styled dark, a black bull, etc. at night. So Apollôn, even by day, when angry is described as νυκτὶ ἐοικώς (*Il.* i. 47); and this simile is also appropriate to all divinities who either bring or suffer death. Thus Assurbanipal describes the death of an enemy by the fine expression, ' He went to his place of Night.'

[4] Vide *sup.* p. 111.

souls of the dead in the Assyrian Hades are compared to birds.

Hêraklês wears ' about his breast an awful belt, a baldric of gold, whereon wondrous things were wrought, bears and wild boars and lions with flashing eyes, and strife and battles and slaughters and manslayings.' The poet gives vent to the curious wish that he who made this belt may never make another. As a mighty work of art we must connect it with the non-Aryan East, and as a matter of fact Euphratean belts and girdles were ' always patterned, sometimes elaborately.' [1] The Nocturnal-sun as Dionysos Nebridopeplos and Hêraklês Astrochitôn wears a starry robe; [2] and if he wears a belt or baldric depending from the shoulder and slanting downwards across the breast to the opposite side, this corresponds in position with and should represent τὴν τοῦ ζωδιακοῦ διάζωσιν. But even if this were so, the poet does not remember or know the fact; and the representations on the belt are not zodiacal. After addressing the hero, Hêraklês retires δόμον Ἀΐδος εἴσω.

Subsection 6. *The Flight of Odysseus.*

And yet Odysseus lingers. Duty is done but curiosity remains; 'I abode there still, if perchance some one of the hero folk besides might come, who died in old time . . . the men of old whom I longed

---

[1] Rawlinson, *Ancient Monarchies,* i. 569.
[2] Vide R. B. Jr., *U.* 78; *sup.* p. 155.

to look on.' What ancient sires, Aryan or Euphratean, wished he to behold? A line, the most suspected in the whole Book, answers Θησέα Πειρίθοόν
τε. According to a tradition given by Plutarch [1]
this passage was inserted by Peisistratos to pleasure
the Athenians. Pausanias, on the other hand, quotes
it as genuine; [2] and the two authorities may pair.
But at all events Homer well knew Peirithoös, 'the
peer of gods in council,' [3] son of Zeus and sire of
Polypoitês, [4] and distinguished as being 'the high-
hearted;' [5] and who, according to old Nestôr, with
Dryas, Kaineus, Exadios and Polyphêmos, surpassed
the best warriors in the host of Agamemnôn. [6]
Panyasis, B.C. 470, who in a late age seems to have
preserved much of the Homerik spirit, related the
daring descent of Thêseus and Peirithoös to the
Underworld; and Polygnôtos in his grand series of
paintings in the Leschê at Delphoi illustrative of the
Eleventh *Odyssey*, placed them together on a throne
not far from the figure of Odysseus. [7] They had also
a joint shrine at Athens. [8] They visited the Shades
in order to carry off Persephonê, [9] and were found
there by Hêraklês in bonds; the great deliverer
rescued Thêseus, Πειρίθουν δὲ, τῆς γῆς κινουμένης,
ἀφῆκεν. [10] The imprisoned Sun (Thêseus) is constantly
rescued from the clutches of Darkness; but Peirithoös

---

[1] *Thêseus*, xx.   [2] Pausanias, X. xxix. 2.   [3] *Il.* xiv. 318.
[4] *Ibid.* ii. 740-1.   [5] *Od.* xxi. 296.   [6] *Il.* i. 262-4.
[7] Pausanias, X. xxix. 2.   [8] Ibid. I. xxx. 4.
[9] Cf. Vergil, *Aeneid*, vi. 393 *et seq.*; Horace, *Carmina*, III. iv. 80.
[10] Apollodoros, II. v. 12.

('Active-effort'), the force which urges it on, is doomed to constantly inhabit and reinhabit the shadowy abode. And Peirithoös is the son of the Ixiôn-sun,[1] so that any apparent confusion or contradiction of idea in the story arises from the separation of the one orb into two distinct personages, one of whom represents his brighter destiny as rising in triumph, the other his darker as ever seeking or dwelling in the gloomy realm, to which he has descended through his love for Persephonê, the beauty-splendour of the universe.[2] According to another version of the story Peirithoös was devoured by the dog Kerberos, the Vedic Sarvari ('Darkness-of-night').

Mr. George Dennis[3] gives a unique representation from a tomb at Tarquinii of Thêseus and Peirithoös with the demon Tuchulcha in the Underworld. 'The hideous and malignant demon, who bears the novel name of *Tuchulcha*, has asses' ears, two hissing snakes bound round his brows and mingling with his shaggy locks,' and 'an enormous eagle's beak, which serves at once for nose and mouth, wide open. He appears to be seizing Pirithous by the neck with one hand, while with the other he brandishes a huge black and blue serpent over the head of Theseus.' He has also 'open wings.' Any explanation of the name *tuchulcha* (= *tu-kul-ka*) will be sought for in vain amongst Aryan dialects; but if we turn to the language of Akkad, the whole occult representation at

---

[1] Apollodoros, I. viii. 1. [2] Vide R. B. Jr., *G. D. M.* i. 278 *et seq.*
[3] *Cities and Cemeteries of Etruria*, edit. 1878, i. 355.

once becomes luminous. *Tu* = (1) the Setting-sun, and hence (2) Darkness (Erebos). *Kul* is ' to destroy ; '[1] and *ka*, ' the mouth.' Tuchulcha would therefore signify in Akkadian ' the Destroying-mouth-of-darkness.' Thus ' the Manducus, a symbolic effigy with gaping jaws, was borne aloft in Roman games and processions to represent the under-world,'[2] ' the jaws of vacant darkness '[3] into which the luckless heroes have fallen, and is a variant phase of the Norse wolf Fenrir and dog Garmr ; but the general idea is naturally not confined to any particular family of the human race. Tuchulcha, like Night, ' embraces with dusky wings.'[4] The question therefore whether the passage *Od.* xi. 631 be spurious, is to some extent doubtful ; and it is in harmony with general mythic legend that Odysseus should desire, and perhaps expect, to meet with Thêseus and Peiri-thoös in the Underworld.

But whilst Odysseus lingers, like Lot in Sodom, ' the myriad tribes of the dead ' throng round with their weird, shrill cries ; and the hero fears, not the ghosts, but ' lest the high goddess Persephonê should send me the head of the Gorgon, that dread monster, from out of Hades.' The myth and history of the terrible lunar Gorgô (' the Swallower '), the devouring darkness which has a bright head—the Moon, I

---

[1] Cf. the Etruscan *kulmu*, the Turkish *ghoul*, etc.
[2] Rev. Is. Taylor, *Etruscan Researches*, 121.
[3] Tennyson, *In Memoriam*, xxxiv.
[4] Vide R. B. Jr., *R. M. A.* 53 *et seq.*

have elsewhere [1] fully related and will not repeat. Its advent Odysseus, the sun now flying to the east, dares not wait ; Luna is still Medousa ('the Ruler '— of the night), and the solar barque speeds onwards towards, and then down the stream of the eastern Ôkeanos, at first labouring with the oar and afterwards ' the fair wind [of morning, Aura-Aurora] was our convoy,' [2] till they came to ' the dwelling place of Dawn and her dancing grounds, and the land of sunrising.' [3] And such is the Homerik history of a day and a night as related in *Od.* xi.

M. Golénischeff has translated a Kemic Papyrus of the XIIth Dynasty which relates the wondrous voyage of an archaic sea-captain, whose travels on sea and shore, according to Prof. Maspero, ' represent the earliest extant specimen of those universally popular tales which relate the adventures of a mortal intruder into the Land of Shadows.' [4] The original intruder, however, is no mortal but a god, the first and greatest of the energizing and labouring heroes, the Sun-god, Hêraklês, Thêseus, Oriôn, Sisyphos, Tantalos, Minôs, Odysseus.

Lastly, we may well agree with Mr. H. F. Tozer in his review of Mr. Bunbury's able *History of Ancient Geography*, that ' the wanderings of Ulysses, when reduced to a scheme, cannot be reconciled with the positions of any actual countries or localities.'

---

[1] Vide R. B. Jr., *U.* sec. vii. Medousa the Gorgô.
[2] *Od.* xi. 636-40.   [3] *Ibid.* xii. 3-4.
[4] Vide Maspero, *Les Contes populaires de l'Egypte ancienne.*

But I equally maintain that these ' wanderings,' even in their very inconsistencies and contradictions, are capable of an absolute and satisfactory explanation in every detail; and that the reasons for the singular statements, beliefs and ideas of the poet may be revealed with crystalline clearness; whilst as regards that portion of the story which is the subject of these pages, I trust the reader will be of opinion that considerable light has been thrown upon a somewhat occult and difficult mythic history.[1]

[1] The subsequent adventures of Odysseus in the Outerworld are not within the scope of the present *brochure.*

THE GREAT DIONYSIAK MYTH.

Vols. I. and II. 8vo. 12s. each.   Eight Illustrations.

'A work of singular research and of bold and original thought.'—STANDARD.

'A mine of careful thought and valuable instruction.'
The Rev. Sir G. W. Cox, M.A., Author of 'Mythology of the Aryan Nations.'

'I hailed your title with delight, which was in no way diminished by my perusal of the opening portions of the work.'—The Right Hon. W. E. GLADSTONE, M.P.

'Mr. BROWN's first volume is an addition to religious mythology. The author treats the question by a "scientific consideration of the historic course of religious thought." There is something fascinating in this first part, which leaves thinking readers impatient to possess the sequel.'—NOTES AND QUERIES.

'This book is characterised by unsparing labour and research, the results of which are stated very clearly, and with the sensibleness that comes of taking a broad view of things. The quantity of material brought together to prove the main argument, that Dionysos was not a deity of Aryan but of Semitic origin, is unparalleled.'
ACADEMY.

'To the task of exploring this field Mr. BROWN has brought a steady resolution and a judicial impartiality which deserve all praise. The admission that Semitic thought and worship exercised some influence on those of the Greeks justifies the attempt to determine, if we can, the character of this influence; there Mr. BROWN has done excellent service. . . . We think that he has fairly proved his main points, that the idea and worship of Dionysos are non-Hellenic and Semitic. In the working out of this subject he has brought together a vast body of most interesting and important matter, and handled it with great skill. Mr. BROWN has fully established his title to our gratitude for a vast amount of solid work already done.'
SATURDAY REVIEW.

'Mr. BROWN has, it must be conceded, fully established his main point. . . . We admit gladly that he has done enough to win for himself a wide and permanent reputation.'—SATURDAY REVIEW (on Vol. II.).

'Le nom de M. ROBERT BROWN, auteur du "Grand Mythe Dionysiaque," est bien connu des mythologues, qui n'ont point oublié ses travaux sur le dieu Poseidon. M. ROBERT BROWN s'est donné pour tâche de déterminer la part qui revient à l'influence sémitique dans la mythologie grecque, et il a trouvé que cette part était considérable. Il surprend des traces d'un élément oriental bien caractérisé dans les rites, dans les idées, et dans les mots. Son livre sur le dieu des mers avait pour but de démontrer que ni le nom, ni la conception de Poseidon, n'avaient une origine hellénique. L'ouvrage qu'il consacre à Dionysos est traité de même dans un esprit d'opposition aux mythologues qui rattachent étroitement le panthéon grec au panthéon védique. . . . Le "Grand Mythe Dionysiaque" est un ouvrage solide autant qu'intéressant.'
BIBLIOTHÈQUE UNIVERSELLE ET REVUE SUISSE.

'The title hardly suggests to an ordinary person the vast amount of ground which the author covers. The Dionysiak Myth, in his view, is nothing less than a picture of all the most important aspects of human life; and mankind, in composing it, may be said, in his words, to have been "revealing their own nature and mental basis." Mr. BROWN has produced two learned volumes, in which the whole matter and many collateral matters are elaborately discussed.'—SPECTATOR.

London: LONGMANS, GREEN, & CO.

'Among the numerous works which the constantly-growing interest in archæology has called forth, Mr. Brown's treatise will be regarded as entitled to high favour. His labours will enable us to read our Bibles and ancient classics more understandingly. He has performed a prodigious deal of hard work, and done it admirably. . . . Dionysos has been selected as the central figure, because his history covers the entire field of research. . . . Mr. Brown brings to his work the charm of novelty, and even of romance. The thoroughness, fidelity, and conscientiousness which he displays are most exceptional.'—The Library Table, New York.

'The story is as interesting as a romance to the archæological inquirer. A profusion of authors are quoted to facilitate the investigation and to substantiate the conclusions. It must be acknowledged that they altogether appear to constitute a very satisfactory explanation.'—The Evolution, New York.

'The Author of the "Great Dionysiak Myth" has given a fuller and more interior view of the fancied grape-god. We are conducted through a world of classical and mythological research far outside of Olympus, and even of Greece, over Syria, Egypt, Arabia, and the far Orient.'—The Medical Tribune, New York.

'During the twelve years which have passed since the publication of the first edition, a large amount of solid work has been done within the domain of comparative mythology. Of the results so gained, probably the most important is the clearer light thrown on the influence of Semitic theology on the theology and religion of the Greeks. This momentous question I have striven to treat impartially; and for my treatment of it I have to acknowledge my obligations to Mr. Robert Brown's valuable researches in the field of the great Dionysiak Myth.'—Rev. Sir G. W. Cox, Preface to the new edition of 'The Mythology of the Aryan Nations.'

London : LONGMANS, GREEN, & CO.

THE RELIGION OF ZOROASTER CONSIDERED IN CONNEXION WITH ARCHAIC MONOTHEISM.

'Mr. Brown is a zealous explorer of the archaic world, and many of his conclusions are new to most classical and other scholars. His monograph on Poseidon clearly shows the non-identity of that divinity with Neptune. The "Great Dionysiak Myth," in like manner, has traced Bacchus from Greece and Egypt to his Assyrian home. The present monograph is also a gem.'—The Medical Tribune, New York.

THE RELIGION AND MYTHOLOGY OF THE ARYANS OF NORTHERN EUROPE.

'As full of learning as of valuable suggestions.'—Rev. A. H. Sayce, Deputy Professor of Comparative Philology in the University of Oxford.

London : E. STANFORD.

LANGUAGE, AND THEORIES OF ITS ORIGIN.

'I have been delighted with what you have written. I know of no other publication in which the present state of the question, in regard to the origin of speech, is presented with so much learning, clearness, and compactness.'—Professor SAYCE.

'Your interesting *brochure* has given me great pleasure. Complete understanding of the weightiness of the problem, and earnest endeavour after truth, is expressed in it.'—Professor LUDWIG NOIRÉ, Mainz.

'I have read your valuable treatise on the Origin of Language with great interest and advantage. It is a very clear and judiciously written chapter of the History of Philology.'—Dr. CARL ABEL, Berlin, Author of 'Linguistic Essays.'

'Mr. BROWN has put together in a very clear and compact form the different theories that have been set forth of late years as to the origin of language. He has gone to the best authorities, and shows a wide extent of reading. At the same time he exercises an independent judgment in regard to the theories he describes, freely criticising those from which he differs. We can thoroughly recommend the pamphlet.'

ACADEMY.

London: E. STANFORD.

THE UNICORN:

A MYTHOLOGICAL INVESTIGATION. With Frontispiece and 5 Illustrations.

8vo. 3s.

'A charming little book, full of learning and instruction.'—Professor SAYCE.

'A delightful excursion into fairyland.'

J. E. TAYLOR, F.L.S., &c. &c., Editor of 'Science Gossip.'

'Mr. BROWN has given us a pleasant, instructive, and original little book. It was a happy thought to impress heraldry into the service of mythology, and show how the arms of England are the last embodiment of an old Aryan legend. Mr. BROWN brings together a vast amount of apt illustration to prove his case. In reading his book we cannot but be struck by the abundant stores of solid learning it displays and the attempt of the Author always to refer to the latest and best authorities. We are led easily and pleasantly on from one point to another, beginning with the art of primæval Babylonia, and ending with the Scottish unicorn, introduced by James I., as the sinister supporter of the royal arms. We must not forget to notice the Scandinavian unicorn, carved on the horn of Ulf, which appropriately forms the frontispiece of the volume.'—ACADEMY.

THE LAW OF KOSMIC ORDER:

AN INVESTIGATION OF THE PHYSICAL ASPECT OF TIME. 8vo. 3s.

'Mr. BROWN comes to the conclusion that the year was regarded by the Accadians as an extended nycthemaron, half the signs being diurnal or relating to the deities of day, and the other half being nocturnal, concerned with myths of the night. Early man thus recognised that there was one and the same law of "Kosmic Order" pervading all conceptions of time. In the course of his investigation Mr. BROWN draws upon Egyptian and Iranian sources, but his chief materiale are necessarily derived from the monuments of ancient Babylonia. . . . We can thoroughly recommend his interesting book to those who care to study a curious chapter in primitive astronomy.'

NATURE.

London: LONGMANS, GREEN, & CO.

'The Author of "The Great Dionysiak Myth" is a laborious student. It seems but yesterday that we noticed his pamphlet on the unicorn, and now we have another book which must have taken, one would suppose, years of study to bring it to its present state of perfection. . . . To us moderns, however ignorant we may be, the idea of time is regulated by a multitude of events of daily and almost hourly occurrence, and but very few of us ever look back to a period when it had to be worked out bit by bit. Mr. BROWN has done this thoroughly well in his own deeply-learned fashion. . . . The book is an important contribution to science, which no future investigator in the same field can afford to overlook.'—NOTES AND QUERIES.

'By Kosmic Order Mr. BROWN means "the harmony of the world in its varied round of day, night, week, month, season, and year." His present work is an attempt to point out the way in which man attained to an idea of this order, so far as the year and zodiacal signs are concerned. It is more especially with the zodiacal signs as we have received them from the Greeks that he concerns himself. They were ultimately derived from the Accadians, who first mapped out the sun's course through the sky, and gave to each section of it the names by which the signs are still, for the most part, known. Mr. BROWN claims to have shown that the signs, when the mythological conceptions which lie at the bottom of them are examined, fall naturally into two groups, six being diurnal and six nocturnal. In this way the year became to early men the day of twenty-four (or rather twelve) hours on an enlarged scale. We always find in Mr. BROWN'S writings proofs of wide reading and happy suggestions. There are very few of his statements with which we should be disposed to quarrel, and the general reader cannot fail to find his work both instructive and interesting.'—ACADEMY.

Recently published.

ERIDANUS, RIVER AND CONSTELLATION:
A STUDY OF THE ARCHAIC SOUTHERN ASTERISMS. With 5 Illustrations on Wood. 4to. price 5s.

CONTENTS:—The Southern Classical Signs—Introduction of the Constellational System from Western Asia—Origin of the Signs of the Zodiac—the Eridanus as connected with the Padus, Nile, Euphrates, and Ocean-stream—the Garden of Eden, Elysium, and Isles of the Blessed—Archaic Constellations of Egypt, China, Palestine, and the Euphrates Valley—the Creation Tablet and Scheme of 36 original Constellations, &c. &c. &c.

'By far the best treatise we have on a most obscure subject.'
                                        NOTES AND QUERIES.

'In reading this *brochure*, one almost stands aghast at the amount of erudition and the extent of research that have been employed in its construction; while the marvellous ingenuity with which the Author has pieced together so many seemingly unconnected facts, drawn from so many various sources, into a logical and convincing series of arguments, all leading to the same conclusion, is not less striking.'
                                        SCOTSMAN.

In preparation.

THE PHAINOMENA, OR 'HEAVENLY DISPLAY' OF ARATOS,
DONE INTO ENGLISH VERSE.

With an Introduction, Notes, and Appendix, and numerous Illustrations from rare Works, MSS., and other sources, of the Constellation-figures and Mythological Personages mentioned in the Poem.

London: LONGMANS, GREEN, & CO.